THE STERLING YEARS

A TRUE STORY

BY BONNIE STERLING

Dick and Bonnie Sterling (Photo by Ray Blasingame)

Hells Canyon Publishing
Halfway, Oregon

Published by Hells Canyon Publishing, Inc., Halfway, Ore.
First printing, December, 1995

Publisher's Cataloging in Publication Data

Sterling, Bonnie,
    The Sterling years / by Bonnie Sterling. — 1st ed. — Halfway, Or : Hells
Canyon Pub., c1995.
    p.   cm.
    ISBN 0-9633919-4-1
    1.Sterling, Bonnie . 2. Snake River Region (Id.)--
        Biography. 3. Frontier and Pioneer Life--Idaho--Idaho County.
I. Title.
    979.57   95-80495

Printed in the United States of America
First Edition

Cover design by Steven D. Backstrom, Hells Canyon Publishing

Cover photo by Gunther Matschke is of Dick Sterling moving a sheep camp through the Seven Devils Mountains of Idaho. When going downhill the mules want to run and must be watched carefully.

DEDICATION

I would like to dedicate this book to Judy Carlson, a very remarkable lady whom I have known for many years. I have never met anyone with more compassion and understanding of life. She has helped me over some rough times in my life, and I want this dedication to be a way of telling her how much I appreciate her friendship and love. I think she will enjoy this story of how I spent a few years of my life.

CONTENTS

LIST OF PHOTOS AND ILLUSTRATIONS

vii

ACKNOWLEDGMENTS

I would like to take this opportunity to thank Verna Slane for the many weekends and evenings she spent editing this document. I began by writing down what I could remember and giving it to JoAnn Lathrop to type into a wordprocessor for Verna to work on. Without the cooperation of these two people this book would never have been finished. I owe them both a debt of gratitude for what they volunteered to do. This is true friendship.

I have many other people to thank for their help in getting all this down on paper: I want to thank, posthumously, the late Albert Crawford of White Bird, Idaho, who gave me the numbers of sheep the herders had in their bands.

A thank you to Gene Hayes of Joseph, Oregon, who drew the picture of our tent house on Slate Creek as I described it. I also want to thank Charles "Jack" Potter, Assistant Park Ranger of Glacier National Park, who gave me a line on the duties we had in our work at the park in 1953.

I must remember to thank Ron Clayton, packer for Fred Harvey, living at Yaqui Point in Grand Canyon, Arizona, who took pictures and reminded me of some of the things I had nearly forgotten about our time spent there. I also thank Russell "Bud" Cooper of Lucile, Idaho, for contributing the Cold Meadows photos as well as Clark H. Neeley, Cuprum, Idaho, for the photos he furnished.

In addition, Johnny Carrey and Ace Barton of Riggins answered my many questions; Bud Cooper identified the picture of the left-handed sheepherders. Ed Vernon provided information and Ray Blasingame sent pictures of Paisley, Oregon.

The poem in the chapter, "The Big One," was written by Robert "Wildhorse" Weister and is used here with his permission.

Last but not least, I must mention George E. "Bud" Wilson, who owned the property at Kirby Creek, Kirkwood, Sheep Creek, Squaw Creek, and the area from Granite Creek to Brush Creek during the time I was on the Snake River. Many thanks to him for giving me the opportunity to have these many exciting adventures to write about and thanks to his daughter, Donna Wilson Matschke, for furnishing the picture on the cover of this book, taken by her husband, Gunther.

I have had an enormous amount of encouragement from all my friends in the Forest Service. I hope they enjoy reading this. All proceeds from this book will go to the BJB Foundation, a nonprofit organization, for scholarship use.

Bonnie Sterling (Bonnie Smith)

PREFACE

This is a true story. When Dick and I met we were both in our twenties. He was born and raised in the West, and I in a large mid-western city. This is the story of how I adjusted from big city life to the back country of Idaho.

I don't pretend to be a writer. It has been difficult remembering the past exactly as it happened. Some things are clear, others dim; some I have positive dates and pictures for. Many of the fall and winter months I grouped together so as not to repeat myself. There are times, places, and different parts of the country I remember, but not the reason we were there or who we were working for. Some years have been omitted because they were not important enough or just didn't fit into the general flow of this story. And some things were better left unsaid.

I was fortunate to have had the opportunity to live on the Snake River in the Hells Canyon area in the years before the dams were built. We enjoyed the excellent fishing for sturgeon and catfish. We watched the Snake River rise to overflowing during high water and drop to low water in the fall. Plenty of drift wood was available and put to good use. I was told the Indian women would pick up small pieces of wood to build their fires, so I imagine the expression "squaw wood" came from that. The large sand bars along the river were great places for trying our luck catching the big one.

10

During high water I've watched trees roll end over end, roots and all. Once the river sucked a very large tree into a whirlpool, shot it straight up out of the water, and swallowed it again. Where or when it surfaced, I never knew.

And so I present to you, the reader, this true story of adventure.

An early photo of Dick Sterling. (Photo donated by Ray Blasingame)

DICK

Dick was born in Oregon but moved to Idaho early in
life. A veteran of World War II, he had served as a nose
gunner in a B-24. When I met him his resemblance to
Bing Crosby was phenomenal. He could have passed for
Bing's twin brother, except he couldn't sing or dance. His
eyes were blue and his hair the blondest ever. At 5 feet,

12

7 1/2 inches, and 155 pounds, he was powerfully strong and well-built with a charm about him that would knock your socks off. Polite and soft spoken, he was exceptionally intelligent with a gift of gab he knew how to use. These qualities saved him many times when he might have gotten into trouble.

He was different. I was thoroughly charmed by him, too much so for my own good, for I never considered what he was actually saying. I was mesmerized.

He was an extremely hard worker and would tackle tough jobs for a chance to achieve where others failed. This boosted his self-confidence.

He was talented but used his talents mainly to benefit himself. He struggled all his life to make a showing for himself, and died before he knew the recognition given his work today. What he wanted most was special recognition from his parents, something he never seemed to achieve.

As for the people he met, he was either liked or instantly disliked. His charm didn't work on everyone but it made a big impression on those he was cultivating for reasons of his own.

He always said he was born fifty years too late for the way he wanted to live and the things he wished to do. He had a strict dress code but hated to dress up. He owned a suit but wore it only to weddings, funerals, and the Masonic Lodge. His hat was dark grey until he decided black was more suited to his coloring. His dress code also applied to me. In fact, he even picked out my clothes—my Levis, boots, and hat.

He loved music and whistled or sang along the trail or at work. He was wonderfully talented as an artist as well. He also loved to read and was especially fond of poems by Robert Service. He even memorized a couple of these poems and would sometimes recite them when around

friends.

He was kind and gentle, but also had a temper when aroused. Then you could hear him for miles around. Never satisfied with things as they were, he was driven by some inner pulse that kept him on the move, always looking for something else. I could never quite figure him out.

I truly loved this man with all my heart even though there were times when I was thoroughly miserable. Of course, we experienced many happy and exciting times which evened up to a life that suited us both.

Dick Sterling, a B-24 nose gunner during World War II

14

An early photo of Bonnie Smith in Rockford, Illinois.
(Photo donated by J. L. Carlson)

BONNIE

I really don't know much about my family's background. I wasn't too interested, and now, when I could use some information, only my brother and I are left. My brother doesn't know as much about the family as I do, since he wasn't interested either.

Now that it is too late to talk to living family members,

15

I decided to try to trace my family history. With the help of Donald P. Brabants of North Easton, Massachusetts, I was able to get a good start. I had heard that I was related to Rutherford B. Hayes, the United States president, but didn't know how.

Through Donnie's research, we found a reference to the Smiths in the book titled "Rutherford B. Hayes and His

Henry A. Smith, Pittsville, Wisconsin, in Civil War uniform.

16

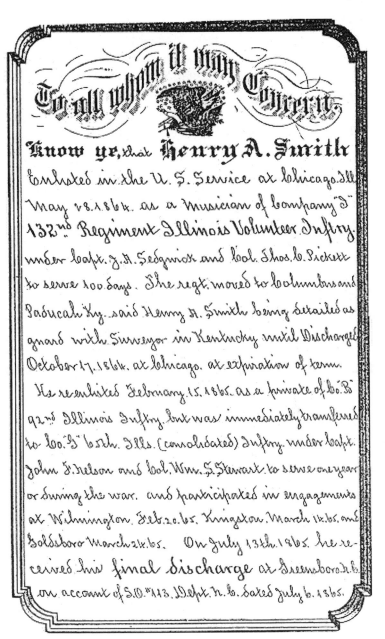

Easel Monument to Henry A. Smith.

17

America" by Harry Barnard, published in 1954.

The Smith connection, we learned, was through Chloe Smith, a descendant of Samuel Smith, the progenitor of probably one fourth of the Smiths in America. Chloe, a sister of my ancestors, was President Rutherford's mother. She was married to Rutherford Hayes, Esq., who, in 1804, was the owner of the Hayes Tavern in Brattleboro, Delaware. The real manager of the tavern, the story goes, was Chloe, a sharp-eyed, stocky woman, a virile, dominant force in the family. Her goal in life was to see each of "Ruddy's" six sisters successfully married.

My grandfather, Henry A. Smith, was a bugler in the Civil War. His bugle and other personal belongings rest in the Midway Village and Museum in Rockford, Illinois.

This picture (page 17) of the stone easel monument was presented to my grandmother, Anna, at the time of my grandfather's death. The monument is an engraved copy of Grandfather's army record, located at a cemetery in Byron, Illinois. It's as readable and well-preserved today as the day it was placed in the cemetery. I do not know who did the engraving or who presented it. My brother visited the site in 1993 to confirm its existence.

Both my parents were born in Illinois, my father in Byron and my mother in Harvard. In my parents' early years their families settled in Rockford. As a young man, my father had a job delivering groceries. He was one of the lucky ones who owned his own team and wagon. My mother's family was one of his customers. In time they met and married.

My brother, sister, and I were born in Rockford. When we were small, my father bought a farm in Argyle and we lived there for a few months. My mother was strictly a city girl and hated the farm, so it wasn't long until we were back in the big city. My father, raised as a farmer, found city life difficult. Finally he found a job as a janitor in an

My parents, Dale and Nina Smith, in Rockford, Illinois, probably on their 25th wedding anniversary.

apartment building. He trained himself to be a painter, plumber, electrician, carpenter, and whatever else was needed to care for the building.

Over the years he found himself janitor of three more apartment buildings. This provided plenty of chores for us kids as we grew up, especially during the summer months. These were depression years so we all had to pitch in and help wherever we were needed.

Once we lived in an apartment in the basement, and it was during this time my father bought a house. For a few years we lived in the apartment for six months in the winter and in the house for six months in the summer. Then my mother showed signs of poor health and we moved into an apartment for good, this time on the third, or top, floor.

Most summers we spent two weeks in Pittsville, Wisconsin, at the farm of my dad's brother, Uncle Julius. None of us really cared to go there because we had to work on the farm just as if we were home, though the chores were different. With seven kids total, things got a little lively at times.

When we returned to Rockford we would have plenty of potatoes and other vegetables for the winter to compensate for our labors. We never went on a regular vacation strictly for the fun of it. There was no money for such things.

I remember when my sister and I were young, my mother's sister would come from Chicago during summer vacation and take us home with her. There we would be all dressed up with nicer clothes than we owned and taken to fancy tea rooms for lunch. My aunt would order a very simple lunch for us, then she would leave. We never worried too much about this practice as we were too impressed with our surroundings. After some time she would return, and, as soon as we had eaten, we went home. This happened several times over a few years. We thought we were the two luckiest girls in the world. Many years later we found out we had been decoys for the Dannenberg Detective Agency. My uncle and his three brothers founded this agency and all worked together.

With the help of my aunt, as well as my sister and me, they had a big part in the capture of Al Capone and in solving this case. We always thought we were being treated as special relatives but that wasn't the case. We were never allowed to take the fancy dresses home with us, but it was exciting to be in Chicago and we had no complaints.

My mother was a concert pianist, and I was taught the piano from the time I could say my abc's. All of us kids had to learn the piano, whether we wanted to or not.

When I was about seven, Andrew Provo, also musically inclined, lived across the street from our summer place. Andrew was from the Hawaiian Islands. We were all quite taken by someone from so far away. He tried to get my brother and sister to learn the ukulele, but they weren't interested. So he taught me to play this instrument and later gave it to me to keep since I had learned to play it. The instrument, of course, came from Hawaii.

When I had mastered the ukulele, he asked my folks to get me a guitar. They finally bought a small one for five dollars. It was second hand, but five dollars was a lot of money to come up with at that time. Andrew Provo taught me to play the guitar; I then played two stringed instruments, as well as the piano.

When I entered junior high school, I signed up for orchestra. They already had a piano player and there was no place in the orchestra for a guitar. My folks put the strings on Grandfather Curran's violin, bought a bow, and I started on that instrument. I was taught the basics during orchestra practice, where I was required to learn to play all stringed instruments. I then started giving beginner piano lessons to pay for my violin lessons.

When I entered high school I was lucky enough to meet a person who gave me the opportunity to play in the Beloit, Wisconsin, symphony orchestra. For the first time

I was getting paid for my playing. All the years of hard work were beginning to pay off.

When we kids were in our early teens my mother formed an orchestra and we played for dances on weekends. My mother, as boss, was on the piano. My brother played the clarinet and saxophone, and I played the violin. My sister, who didn't want to learn an instrument, was our vocalist. Against her will, I'm sure. We hired a drummer, the only one who was paid for playing, as we kids never saw any money that my mother received. We were relieved when she called the whole thing off. It was too much work and took too many weekends. What with school, our music, and our chores, we were kept plenty busy without having all our weekends taken.

We did have some play time and my favorite pastime was western movies. My folks didn't like us going to movies, but we'd sneak off whenever we had the chance. I especially liked the ones with Bob Steele. And then there was Hopalong Cassidy and, I guess, others.

When I watched a western movie I would pretend I was the girl on the horse. I thought it would be heavenly to ride across the countryside like that. I knew it was a dream and the only horses I ever saw were on farms.

I did have a friend who rode his horse from Rockford to some place in Wyoming one summer to work as a cowboy on a ranch. The distance was over 2,000 miles, but at that time I didn't realize just what he had accomplished.

One time my favorite Bob Steele movie was coming to the theater for a Saturday matinee. I had no money and neither did my friends. We came up with the idea of stealing milk bottles off back porches and cashing them in at the store to get the five cents we needed for the movie. And that's exactly what we did. Then, using the excuse of going to the library to study, we took off for the movie. No money for bus or treats, but we were all in high spirits.

About half way through the movie I began to realize what we had done. The more I thought about it the worse I felt. I paid less attention to the movie, wondering if anyone had seen us take the milk bottles. I knew my dad would have a punishment far greater than any ever known before. I could hardly sit and wait for the finish of the movie, afraid to go home and afraid not to. When I got home nothing was said. We got by with it that time, but I decided there must be a better way of raising money for movies. It was the last time any of us did that.

After graduation, I continued playing in the symphony and worked in an appliance store. I had not taken any secretarial courses to prepare for an office job. Instead I had taken only the required subjects plus music appreciation, harmony, orchestration, and, as a foreign language, Spanish. I thought I would be an interpreter and, that way, pay for music lessons. There was no opening at the time for an interpreter so I had to take the store job. I worked six days a week from 9 a.m. until 6 p.m., earning seven dollars a week. All I had to do was answer the phone and test radio tubes. No experience was needed.

When I got bored with that job, I got another, clerking at the candy counter in Walgreen's drugstore. I got so sick of the smell of hot chocolate from the heat of the lights, that I quit that job, too. Then I worked for the telephone company for awhile. So far I wasn't doing very well and realized I hadn't taken the right studies in school.

My mother's health was failing and things seemed to be getting worse. The only thing going for me was my music, but I couldn't make a living at that. In time my mother passed away and I seemed at a loss for what to do. I didn't know anything but city life and had no thought of living anywhere else. Now, in my early twenties, I felt a complete failure at everything I tried to do.

Then a letter came from an aunt who lived in Oregon. She had heard about my mother's death. After that letter arrived, I decided what I needed was a change of scenery. So I wrote to my aunt asking if I could come for a visit. The reply was affirmative. I took what money I had saved and bought a bus ticket to Oregon. I had never traveled anywhere by myself. My family was opposed to my going, but I knew I had to do it.

By this brief description of my early life it is clear I was familiar with city sidewalks, buses, street cars, taxis, heated apartments, hot and cold running water, and a modern bathroom. Having anything other than these modern conveniences was never in my scheme for the future. I would later find out I had a lot of learning yet to do. I wasn't as grown up as I thought I was. Paisley, Oregon, was a long way from Illinois.

I would have enjoyed the trip out West more if I hadn't been so timid. I was afraid to talk to anyone, kept to myself, and was very glad when it was over.

OREGON

As I stepped off the bus in Lakeview, I was met by Aunt Blanche and Uncle Earl. I had never met my uncle before, and had only seen Aunt Blanche once when she made a trip to Rockford many years earlier.

On the ride to Paisley we became acquainted and I enjoyed seeing new country, a kind of country I had never known before. I saw cattle that were different from those I had been used to seeing in a state with lots of dairy cows. I was excited and pleased with myself for making this decision.

Paisley was a quiet, western town like you'd see in a Western movie. It had a hotel with a bar and cafe where the meals were served family style. It had two gas stations and two garages. Then there was the Bannister Cafe, Cooley's Pool Hall and Bar, Bennefield Hall, the school house, post office and Masonic Hall. A general merchandise store and some cabins to rent rounded out the town. About 400 people lived there at that time.

One of the biggest ranches in the area was the ZX, run by the Chewaucan Land and Cattle Company and supervised by Buster Vaughn. Miller and Lux owned the ranch and ran 19,000 head of cattle plus bulls and horses on about 2,200 square miles spread across southern Oregon.

Actually, I only remember a few special places from when I was in Paisley in the 40s. The details come mostly from Ed Vernon of Milton-Freewater, Oregon, who was born and raised in Paisley.

I had been in town a couple of days when Aunt Blanche mentioned a dance at the school on Saturday night. I wasn't particularly interested in going, but it was one of the main social events around there and everyone from all over the area would be there.

This was my first real country dance. Several years before, my sister and I had gone to some of Sidney Smith's elegant barn dances. He was famous for the cartoon strip, Andy Gump. But those dances were nothing compared to this dance. This was *real country*.

Because I was a stranger visiting from the East, I was the most popular girl at the dance. I was surrounded by cowboys, ranch hands, and all the other single men. I had never had so much attention in my life. I had many invitations for the auctioned lunch, but finally settled on the one who asked first.

At intermission several of us went outside and as many as possible climbed into a car. We were all laughing and talking and just having the best time, when the door of the car opened. I was sitting in the middle of the front seat with a new cowboy friend on each side. The person who opened the door was the blondest, most handsome man I had seen in many a day. By the time he was introduced to me as Dick Sterling, I was wishing I was alone.

He worked on the ZX Ranch the same as the other cowboys but they were surprised to see him. He had ridden his horse in from the ranch like most of the others, even though earlier, he had decided to forego the dance. He had planned to have a long ride the next day. He said that, after everyone had gone, the bunkhouse got too quiet and he changed his mind.

About that time the music started again. Dick asked me to dance, but I was spoken for. When it came time to

auction off the lunches the ladies had brought, I was again spoken for. Up until this time, I'd had no dances with this handsome cowboy. When the dance started again I finally made time available for him. He wasn't the best dancer, but he was sure popular with the girls.

After that first dance, we danced every dance until it was over. He wouldn't let anyone else cut in. I was in seventh heaven. Of all the girls in the schoolhouse, he had picked me. Not only did he have beautiful light blonde hair, his blue eyes actually sparkled. Or maybe the sparkle was in my own eyes. I think right then and there I fell madly in love with him.

The dance lasted until daylight and everyone went home. Most slept away the day, but the cowboys had to go to work. I had never had such an experience and no one had ever made such a fuss over whether I danced or not. My life was taking on a new twist. Here was a real, live cowboy, just like the movies, and I had met him. There were others at the dance but this was the one and only.

A couple of days later Dick came to the house and asked me if I would go to a basketball game with him that evening. He had ridden his horse in from the ranch.

I agreed to go. He tied his horse to the power pole in front of the house and we walked to the school where the game was being played. From then on, for the time I was there, we went to all basketball games in the area. And we went by car to those out of town, since a few cowboys owned cars. We attended every dance, too, although there weren't many, as I wasn't there very long. Less than three weeks to be exact. Imagine, my cowboy coming to town on his horse to see me. I just couldn't believe all this was happening to me.

After sixteen days had passed I knew I could stay no longer. I dreaded telling Dick, and dreaded worse having to leave. I knew nothing would ever be the same in my life again. I waited a day or so more and when Dick came to town I told him I was leaving the next morning as my two week stay had passed and I could stay no longer. I told him I was leaving for Boise, Idaho, on the stage in the morning. He didn't say much and I couldn't have been more miserable.

Next morning, when I got on the stage, there he was. He had quit his job and was going first to Boise and then on to where his folks lived in New Meadows north of Boise in the mountains. We had a long time to visit on the bus. By the time we arrived in Boise we had decided to go to Reno, Nevada, and get married. I couldn't believe my ears. I agreed, but also told him I had to return to Illinois to tell my family and tie up loose ends.

We returned to Boise immediately after being married where I boarded the train for Illinois, and he went on to New Meadows, Idaho, to his folks' place. It was two weeks before I returned. Dick borrowed his Dad's pickup, met me in nearby McCall when the bus arrived, and took me to New Meadows and the Circle C Ranch where his folks lived and worked.

In the meantime Dick had gotten a job with the U.S. Forest Service. So our first job was not on a ranch like I'd thought. Nothing had ever been said about working on a ranch. Nothing at all had been said, for that matter. I had jumped to conclusions.

Idaho, South Fork of the Salmon

As a Forest Service employee, Dick would be in McCall for a couple of weeks. We would live in a Forest Service cabin while Dick attended fire school and received instructions for his summer duties.

I learned he would be the packer taking salt to the salt licks, clearing trails, and packing supplies to lookouts in his area. He would also shoe his own stock and pack supplies to fires, if there were any. When there was a fire, the firefighters would be trucked as near as possible. Then they would put on backpacks, pick up their tools, and walk to the fire. While we werc in McCall I enjoyed the beautiful scenery and the leisure days. My only worry was what to cook for the next meal, as I was a poor cook. In a few days Dick told me we would be leaving soon for the Forest Service guard station on the South Fork of the Salmon River where he would be stationed for the summer.

He told me to make out a grocery list for three months. I had no idea how to make out a list for even a week, let alone three months. Since I didn't know how, I did nothing. That night, when he came home, he asked me about the grocery list. I just said, "I forgot, I'll do it tomorrow."

The next day it was the same thing. Finally he said the list had to be done as we would be leaving at the end of the week. I had to admit I didn't know how. He grabbed a piece of paper and a pencil and, after a barrage of cuss words, sat down and wrote the list himself. He should have done it in the first place, but then I should have admitted I didn't know how. In those few days I realized my true love had a temper and knew a lot of cuss words, some I had never heard before. I was learning, but if I thought these last few days were bad, it's a good thing I didn't know what the summer was going to bring.

The morning we were to leave we went to the store and bought everything on his list and more. That time in the store made up for some of the rough times of the previous days. After everything was loaded in a Forest Service truck, we headed out. If I remember correctly, Bill Parks drove us to the Guard Station. The conversation between Bill and Dick was way out of my reach. I didn't have a clue as to what they were talking about. But the scenery was beautiful and I was really enjoying myself.

As I looked out at what surroundings I could see through the windshield, I marveled at the beauty. As the time and the miles went by, however, I began to concentrate less and less on the scenery and more and more on the road, which was getting much narrower. It was so much narrower that sometimes I wondered if all four wheels were still on it. I'd never been on a road like this. I was scared to death but couldn't say a word. I thought I'd met my Maker a time or two when another vehicle came toward us, but we always made it past. By the time we reached Secesh (pronounced see-sash) Summit I was so scared I was just barely there and no more. What a relief when we stopped at Warren. I thought we had reached our destination until I found out we had more miles to travel.

How in heaven's name did I get myself into this fix? Easy. By falling in love.

If I thought the road to Warren was bad, I hadn't seen

the road to the South Fork yet. It was dusk by the time we reached the guard station. I was so miserable I didn't care where we were. Two fellows at the station helped unload the truck. After supper, which the men had prepared, the two fellows left with Bill Parks and I couldn't believe the day was finally over.

South Fork Guard Station on the South Fork of Salmon River. Johnny Carrey, co-author of "Snake River of Hells Canyon," lived here as a child before his father sold the property to the U.S. Forest Service.

The next morning Dick got up, built a fire, and cooked breakfast. The world wasn't such a bad place after all. We spent the day putting our groceries away. There was a wonderful cinderblock cellar, which served not only as a cellar, but as a haven when the weather got hot in August. We left the door of the cabin open at night and closed it during the day. There was a screen door to keep animals, snakes, and insects from getting in. Our potatoes, carrots, onions, and eggs kept all summer. The next few days were wonderful, and I was beginning to think this wasn't such a bad deal after all. The scary road and long ride were forgotten.

31

The guard station was made of logs with five sparsely furnished rooms. The floors were hardwood throughout. Two bedrooms had nothing in them. The third had a bed and chest of drawers. The big living and dining room had a round, wooden dining table and four chairs. The large windows let in a lot of light, but had no curtains. I *eventually* got used to that.

A telephone switchboard stood on legs along one wall. It was just big enough to handle all the lines necessary for use in the back country. The regulation Forest Service desk had a wooden top that lifted up to access the storage underneath. Dick did his paperwork and diary entries there.

In the kitchen a big wood cookstove occupied one wall. There was a small kitchen table and two wooden chairs. It was convenient to have running water in the kitchen, even though hot water had to be heated on the stove. There was a big porch on the front and an equally big one in back.

Two round washtubs and the washboard hung on the back of the house. We were well-supplied with candles and a couple of kerosene lamps, two Coleman lanterns with mantles, as well as generators and gas. But where were all the modern conveniences I was so used to?

The yard, with lots of fruit trees, was fenced in. It was heavenly. This had been the house where Johnny Carrey of Riggins was born and lived as a small child. His parents had sold it to the Forest Service. It was one of the nicest places to live, so I was very fortunate in that respect.

Dick did most of the cooking the first few days, so things went smoothly. Then came the evening when he said to me, "Tomorrow morning you will get up and build a fire and make coffee." He explained carefully how it was done. He whittled the kindling, placed it in the stove, put some larger wood on top, and added a bigger piece. Then

South Fork Guard Station fenced-in pasture below the station.

he said, "This is the damper. This way it's open, and this way it's closed."

I listened carefully and was sure I would have no problems. Then he took everything out of the stove, so I'd have to start from the beginning.

I really thought I had it down pat so I went to bed and slept like a log. The next morning I got up, dressed, and went to the kitchen. I put the kindling in first, a little bigger piece, then a nice big one, and lit a match. The pitch blazed quickly. I shut the door, took the coffee pot, filled it with water, and then looked at the stove again. Lo and behold, the kindling had burned, then gone out.

Then I remembered the damper. Now was it open or closed? What had Dick said? I just couldn't remember. And I thought it was going to be so easy. He was still in bed. It wasn't long before he started yelling, wanting to know if the coffee was ready yet. And I still had a cold stove. I took everything out and, with the butcher knife, tried and tried to whittle some kindling. I just didn't have the knack. It looked so easy when Dick did it. I began to bawl and plead with the stove to please burn. I had opened and closed the draft so many times I couldn't remember where it was supposed to be, up or down.

Finally Dick got up and came out to the kitchen madder than a wet hen, using cuss words I hadn't heard before. I can tell you now, that was the last time he ever had to show me how to build a fire. I never forgot again.

Things went pretty smoothly for a day or two and then Dick said he had to go to Pilot Peak to get the pack string which was running loose with the bell mare. We had a couple of horses at the station. Both belonged to Dick. I was finally going to get to ride a horse. I was thrilled. Imagine, all my dreams were coming true.

He saddled the mare, Babe, for me, since I didn't know how, and then gave me strict instructions on what to do. There were so many instructions I couldn't remember them all. One thing he kept repeating was that when we got to the head of the trail I was to stay there and turn the pack string down the trail. "And," he said, "under no circumstances are you to get off your horse. Do you understand?"

I said okay, and off we went. What I didn't realize was that, since Dick was riding a half-broke gelding, he would have his hands full without having to stop and help me back on my horse. He hadn't bothered to explain why it was so important for me not to get off.

The long, leisurely ride up to the clearing where you could look up and see the lookout was wonderful. As we rode I began to think the world was a pretty good place after all. Riding a horse was a snap. I had no problems. I was really enjoying the day. Of course it was all uphill which is easier riding. I thought, after the episode with the stove, I had finally entered the summer's paradise.

When we reached the clearing where I was supposed to sit on my horse and wait for the pack string, Dick repeated, "You sit right here on your horse. When the mules come down towards you, turn them down the trail." And again, "Don't get off your horse."

That was fine with me. I could look up the country and see the lookout and was glad I didn't have to ride up there. Babe was a 23 year-old, supposedly gentle mare. She grazed around, staying in about the same spot.

Then, in the far distance, I heard a bell. So did Babe. The closer it got, the worse she got, and then I didn't think too much about riding horses. My wonderful day was not wonderful any more. The tranquility of the mountain top turned to terror. Babe danced, she pranced, she threw her head and did all the things I didn't know a horse could do. I was terrified.

As the bell got even closer, Babe decided she was going to join the other stock and I couldn't hold her. So I did what I was told not to do. I slipped off her back and stood in front of her.

When the mules and Dick came pell-mell down the hill, the mules and bell mare turned down the trail like they were supposed to. Only one thing was wrong. I had gotten off my horse. Dick's gelding was wanting to run with the others. He had a heck of a time calming the horse down enough to get off him and help me on my horse. Talk about one mad cowboy. I got the cussing of my life. He just left me and rode off down the trail after the stock. I walked the mare slowly down the trail as it was not as smooth going downhill as up.

Lucky for me, when the mules got to the guard station, they stopped to graze and Dick was able to run them into the corral. I rode in quite a few minutes later, hating myself, the horse, Dick, and the whole country. I found a very cool cowboy, and I wondered if I would ever learn to ride a horse. I wasn't as thrilled about it as when we left that morning.

Thinking about the trials and tribulations with the stove, and then with the horse, I was wondering if I had made a poor choice in picking a cowboy. But it must have been trying to Dick, who was an excellent horseman, to have a wife who was such a greenhorn. He kept forgetting I didn't know anything about anything. There was more than one time when I wondered what had happened to the attentive cowboy I had danced with at Paisley. Somewhere along the line I had lost track of him. Maybe he was still there with me, only this was real life, not a dance hall.

We rode almost every day the rest of the summer, and I had better luck most of the time. After that first session, Dick took the time to show me how to mount a horse and how to handle it when unusual things happened. I didn't learn it all in a day or all in one summer, but it was a beginning. I still wasn't much of a rider, and I surely didn't glide over the countryside like movie cowboys did.

Time marched right along. There were many things to be done at the guard station during the summer. I was given the chore of recording the weather twice a day and calling it into McCall. We had the switchboard to operate, a chore that was mine, too.

We were living in one of the most beautiful settings I had ever seen. I was very happy, except for the times I pulled a boner, which was quite often. Seems like I was crying over some dumb mistake all summer long. But I guess that's the way you learn. It just seemed to be taking me longer to learn than it should have.

When the first wash day came I was given the washboard and told to use it. Now I had never used a washboard before and, although I used it every week, I never got the knack of it. I had raw knuckles all summer long.

As the summer wore on I tried to learn to cook the

things that Dick liked to eat. One day he told me to cook some red beans for supper, something else I had never done. I had never before seen or cooked red beans, or any other kind of dried beans, so I fell back into the old groove of, "I forgot." I still had the habit of saying that rather than admit I didn't know how.

When Dick got in that night, he took the beans and sorted them, taking out the rocks. Now if I had done the job, there would have been rocks in the beans, so it was a good thing I didn't do it. Sometimes I lucked out.

Like I said, we heated our wash water and bath water on the stove or by the sun during the hottest part of the summer. That way we didn't have to build a fire during the heat of the day. Dick was gone at least two days a week, and I was content to enjoy learning to cook. We had some neighbors a couple miles or so away, and one of them, Betty, would call me on the phone and read a recipe to me. She taught me to make sourdough, but I didn't do anything with that information until many years later.

When the Transparent apples were ripe we had apples fixed in some way as long as they lasted. We shared with the birds and deer. With our three months supply of groceries, we didn't have extra sugar for things like candy. Sugar was for daily use, and since neither Dick nor I used sugar in coffee or tea, I made pies, sauces, and cookies.

Bacon, I was to find out through the years, was the main meat for all meals. So it was for our meals that summer. It was a wonderful seasoning for the kinds of foods we were eating. I had never eaten meals like I was learning how to prepare, tasty meals out of cans. We used canned meats and did very well. My cooking was far from gourmet, but I was trying. I learned how to write a grocery list, too.

The woodstove and I weren't very good friends. I still

37

needed to learn more about what made it function. Everything was either burned or not done enough. The fire was either too hot or too cold. If I ever got it the right temperature, it was by accident. I moved the pots and pans constantly to find the right spot on the top of the stove. I trimmed burned edges off biscuits and anything else I baked in the oven.

I didn't have a measuring cup or spoons. What recipes I had, I had to guess at the measurements. Thank goodness boiled potatoes were popular. As for frying potatoes, I had a frightful time. Standing over the stove and trying to keep the right amount of wood in it posed almost insurmountable problems the first few weeks.

Whenever possible, I opened a can. When I failed completely, I walked a long way from the house and tossed the failure so that the birds would eat it and Dick wouldn't know I had wasted food. The animals and birds ate pretty well.

Then there was the episode with the coffee pot. When I first started to make boiled coffee, I noticed the inside of the pot had never been scrubbed. So I took it upon myself to bring the inside of the pot to its original color, a nice grey enamel. I scrubbed and scrubbed until it was shiny clean. I thought I'd done something great but when Dick went to make the next pot of coffee he was furious. I learned you just dump out the grounds, rinse it out, and it's ready for the next pot. I learned it wasn't for me to make decisions about the way things were done in the house either.

It's not clear to me just when it became a little easier to prepare a meal. By the time the end of the summer came along I was doing pretty well with what went into the oven. Really nothing to brag about, but much, much better than when I started.

I was tired of being reminded of how I talked. If I was

going to stick it out in this part of the country, I'd better start speaking like they did. First I practiced dropping my "g's." Now that isn't the easiest thing to do when you've been trained to pronounce all the letters in a word. Riding became "ridin'" and looking became "lookin'." I wanted to do something that would please Dick, if possible. When I ran out of things to do during the day, I spent many an hour rolling Bull Durham cigarettes.

I also remember the time I came back from recording the weather and told Dick there was a rattlesnake curled up under a tree root at the spring. He asked if I'd killed it and I said, "No." He took me right out the door, grabbed a hoe, and marched me back out to the spring. The snake was still curled up in the same spot. Dick made me take the hoe and kill it. It took some doing, I can tell you for sure. I was lucky, though, because the snake had just swallowed a rodent and was too stuffed to move. I killed it several times over, but finally learned the knack of using a hoe to kill snakes. There were lots of them around the guard station, so it was a lesson well-taught and learned.

Since we had no electricity, we amused ourselves by reading what books were in the cabin. Along with his other talents, Dick was an artist. He would draw a horse in several different positions which, when rolled on a pencil, looked like it was running. He had a secret desire to work for Walt Disney and draw cartoons. If the Disney studio had been somewhere in the back country he might have spent more time drawing horses than riding. He loved horses and there were very few times in his life when he wasn't working with them in some way.

Dick also liked to sing. He knew the words of some old cowboy songs and he taught them to me. One in particular that I remember was called "Yavapi Pete." I can remember it to this day. I never heard it anywhere except when Dick sang it.

As I mentioned earlier, the yard around the house was fenced. There was also a fenced-in pasture which included the house and yard. When Dick wrangled the stock he made me stand between the house and the fence. When they came running towards me, I was to wave my arms and yell so they would stop and stay put. That was one thing I failed at completely all summer. I never got up courage to stand my ground when they were running pell-mell towards me. It was temper-tantrum time every day he needed the pack string. Some things I thought I would never learn, and now I can't remember when I didn't know them. A time or two during the summer when Dick didn't need my horse, he would saddle her for me and I would ride the few miles to the neighbors to visit for a few hours. I still wasn't much of a rider. Since I kept the horse at a walk, I had plenty of time to scan the road and countryside, hoping nothing unexpected would happen. I knew if ever I had to get off my horse, it would be a walk home.

There were many things that had to be done each day, so I had a routine of sorts. That made the time go faster when Dick was gone all day. One time Dick left and said he'd be back before dark and to be sure to have supper ready. It was going to be a long day.

He was never one to take a lunch, always figuring he'd be back sooner than he stated. It didn't always work out that way. As the day wore on and he didn't come in and he didn't come in, I began to worry. Then it was dark. I would have to light the Coleman lantern. I had never had to do it all summer as Dick had always came in before dark. He had told me how to light it once, but time had passed and, since I didn't think I would ever have to do it, I just didn't worry about it.

I was too ashamed to call Betty on the phone, not

wanting to admit my ignorance. So I took the lantern and pumped it up as best I could. Then I thought, "How do you shut it off without losing the air when you take your thumb off the hole?" Remember, I'm a dumb city kid trying to learn a million things all in a few weeks. I was scared to death of the hissing of the lantern anyway. I finally decided I would just as soon take a good cussing. I gave up, let the fire go out in the cook stove, and went to bed. Not to sleep, of course.

At eleven thirty that night Dick came in tired and hungry. You can imagine what went through his mind when he saw a dark house. His stock always came first, so when he had them all taken care of he came yelling into the house. I did my darnedest to play dead, and wished I was. Things slam-banged around the kitchen. Next day was a gloomy one, and I had another lesson on how to light a gas lantern, which I never forgot again.

Dick didn't have temper tantrums. He just lost his temper and cussed. I'm the one who stamped my foot and yelled. He would get so disgusted with me for calling everything "dang" this or that, "heck," "golly darn," and so on. One day he said to me "If you are going to get that mad at something say, "Damn," "Hell," or call it an "S.O.B."

Now notice, he said "something" not "someone." Anyway, later he did something which infuriated me. I thought for once I'd remember what he had told me and I'd be doing something right for a change. So I turned to him and called him an S.O.B. Except these words were not abbreviated. I said them clearly and distinctly.

Well, everything changed fast. He grabbed me, turned me over his knee, grabbed a stick of wood out of the wood box, and gave me a whipping I can feel yet. Then I really got mad since, for once, I'd done something he'd told me to do.

When tempers calmed, he had to explain to me why he got so mad. I learned another lesson the hard way. I learned to listen to what he actually said and not go off half-cocked. That was the only time he ever gave me a whipping. He probably felt like it at times though.

Sometimes the stock ran loose around the station. We blocked the trails and put logs across the bridge so they couldn't cross. We used Babe for odd jobs. One job was to hook her to the stone boat and keep the road free of the large rocks the mules, horses and deer knocked loose to roll onto the road. That was lots of fun and I enjoyed helping Dick. It doesn't take smarts to put a rock in a stone boat but it took some doing to control Babe, who wasn't too fond of the task. Especially when all of the rest of the stock were free.

The mail was delivered once a week, a nice diversion. Neighbors came to visit once in a while, and I talked to some who were stationed on lookouts in the area. I think right then and there is when I unconsciously made up my mind I'd like to live in a place like this forever. The quiet and solitude were impressive and, at times, soothed my frayed nerves.

Towards the end of August, Dick had places to go with the pack string and I couldn't go. One of the days when he was gone I ventured into the Forest Service barn where many things were stored. I had no idea what they were except for the many fire packs all lined up and ready to go, maybe two hundred.

I don't remember hearing anything about forest fires in my early years. And if I had heard, I had no idea what they were like or what the Forest Service did about them.

After that first day at the big barn, I went most every time I was alone. I never mentioned these things to Dick as I wasn't sure I was supposed to go in there.

Then one day I opened one of the packs and looked

inside. I didn't touch anything, just looked. Then curiosity got the better of me. The next time I opened a pack from the very last row. I took everything out and read the labels and put them all back just like they were. But I kept remembering the ration that said there was a chocolate candy bar inside.

I stayed away from temptation for awhile, but finally went back and opened the same pack and took out the box with the candy bar in it. Now I was old enough to know better, but maybe things were going too smoothly. In time, I stole the candy bar and ate it very slowly. I really enjoyed it, thinking to myself that no one would miss it. Before fire season started I had eaten four. Then I began to worry. What if there was a fire and all the packs were taken out? They would know someone had taken the candy.

I was more than unhappy about what I had let myself do, and I knew Dick would next to kill me if he knew.

Although I had always loved storms, I now had more reason to worry about fire danger. I liked to hear the thunder and watch the lightning dance along the phone line as it rang the bells on the switchboard. But now, every time there was a storm, I worried about the lightning and hoped there would be no fires. I never went back to the barn the rest of the time I was there.

One day, after something I had done wrong, Dick and I had a violent quarrel. I decided it was time for me to leave. I went out to the horse barn, caught my mare, Babe, and tied her in the stall. I curried her and put on the blanket. Then it was the saddle. Dick's saddle was too heavy for me to lift. I tried and tried. I finally got up on a box and tried to lift the saddle to the back of the horse. How I thought I was going to lift the saddle any better standing on the box, when I couldn't lift it when I was on the ground, is beyond me. But when you're mad you don't think straight.

I struggled and struggled and the more I tried, the madder and more determined I got. Then all of a sudden I heard uproarious laughter. When I turned around Dick was looking through the logs, laughing at me. He came in the barn and said if I wanted to leave so bad, he'd saddle the horse. Then he reminded me it was ninety miles to McCall and would take several days to ride there. I gave up, admitting I was wrong. I sure hated to do that.

Then came the day there was a fire. I decided it was time for me to leave. This time it was the right thing to do, as firefighters were coming in, and Dick would be busy with the pack string. So I packed my clothes and rode in a Forest Service truck back to McCall to live in a Forest Service cabin and wait for Dick to finish his job.

The summer was a strange one for me. I had so many mixed feelings. I would be soaring in the clouds one minute or sinking below bottom the next. Looking back, it seems like I spent the whole summer crying about something I did wrong. Then I had to deal with my temper tantrums. I was trying to learn a lifetime of lessons in one three-month span. Dick couldn't remember that I was an ignorant city girl, and it took more than one lesson or demonstration for me to grasp what I was supposed to know or do. I sometimes would wonder why I was there, but then it always came down to the fact that I dearly loved Dick, regardless. Love is not only blind, but stupid as well.

After all was said and done I figured it would be better to be miserable part of the time with him, than to be miserable all the time without him. Either way, I wasn't going to win, but given time maybe I could learn to be a better wife. I had a lot of growing up to do. Many days were wonderfully happy. All I had to do was stop and remember that not everything I was doing would turn out to be wrong. At least I would stick it out and see what would happen after we were back in civilization.

So ended my first summer in the back country. I wondered how I had ever lived through it. Still, I was looking forward to doing it again with quite a bit more knowledge than when I started.

GARY COOPER

When Dick's job was over with the Forest Service we went to New Meadows to visit his folks. While there, he was contacted by Larry Garner, who had a hunting and fishing guide service in the primitive area of Idaho. Larry wanted Dick to pack hunters for him at Cold Meadows and Chamberlain Basin.

I stayed with Dick's folks at the Circle C Ranch. Dick didn't stay very long with Larry because he came down with the flu, but he would work for Larry again in the years to come and I would go with him.

When he recovered, we went to Boise. I worked as a waitress at the Idanha Coffee Shop and Dick found work tending bar. That way of life lasted only a few weeks. Dick was fed up with city life and we returned to New Meadows.

One afternoon, when nothing very exciting was happening at home, we walked up to the New Meadows Hotel and Bar. When we entered the bar we had a delightful surprise. At the bar sat Allen Wilson, Dick's friend from Granite Creek on the Snake River. Beside Allen was Gary Cooper. Allen had taken Gary on a late fall bear hunt. He didn't get a bear, but seemed very pleased with the hunt and the chance to see the country again. Allen's son, Kim, told me Gary had been into Granite Creek many times, as Allen and Gary were old friends. There weren't very many people in the bar since no one knew this famous actor was in town.

No one wanted to leave and miss out on the conversation. He was friendly, soft spoken, and just like any other guy. We were all quite taken with him. He was on his way back to California and they had just stopped in the bar to have a drink before going their separate ways. I always had a soft spot in my heart for Gary Cooper after that.

Knights Ferry, California

Dick decided he wanted to winter in California. We didn't have a car, so we left on the bus with one suitcase, his saddle, and tack. We got off the bus in Sacramento and rented a hotel room. After supper we spent the evening on the phone calling number after number trying to find a cattle ranch.

What we got was a prune ranch, walnut ranch, grape ranch and every other kind of ranch in that area except one with cattle. So we decided to visit Dick's friends who lived in Coarsegold. We stayed with Ike and Clara Blasingame for awhile. Ike was working for the RO Cattle Company. Since Dick was looking for a job cowboying, it wasn't long before he was hired.

The boss, George Wiswall, took us to Merced, south of Modesto. He helped us sign into a hotel room and told Dick he would see him in the morning. Dick was awakened at 4 a.m. As he left he said, "I'll see you tonight."

All the money we had in the world was in Dick's pocket. I wasn't too worried about not having money as I smoked Bull Durham cigarettes, drank plenty of water and thought about the big meal I would eat that night. Well, he didn't come back that night nor the next night. On the evening of the third day he returned.

During that time I got real hungry. I did not have the proper clothes to get a job as a waitress and no money to buy any. I tried to sleep as much as possible but, when

Bonnie Sterling at Coarsegold, California. (Photo donated by R. Blasingame)

your stomach is empty, it's hard to do. I would have been put out of the hotel if George hadn't been with us when we registered. The old gal knew she would get her money when he returned. She didn't give a darn about me.

The first thing George said to me when he found out I'd been without money was, "Why didn't you call my wife?" I didn't because I didn't know he had a wife and I didn't have a dime. I survived the ordeal, but that was the last time all the money in the family was in one pocket.

The next day George took us to Knights Ferry, to one of his ranches. We'd be there all winter. This little town, as I remember, had a store with a liquor section in it, a post office, a tavern-cafe, a grocery store, and a gas station. A covered bridge spanned the Stanislaus River.

Finally I was going to live on a ranch. All the things I thought we were going to do in our life together were coming true. Knights Ferry was a very pretty part of the country. The ranch was wonderful. We had a small, three-room house with a bath and the now familiar woodstove. The only thing wrong was that it had no furniture except for a kitchen table and two chairs.

Dick and Bonnie Sterling at the mining town of Coarsecold before going to work for the RO Cattle Company at Knight's Ferry. (Photo donated by R. Blasingame)

George told us to take the ranch truck the next day to Oakdale and get some furniture. And so we did! We went to a second-hand store and got a bed, springs, mattress, davenport and chair, some towels, sheets, and other things including a few dishes, pots and pans and whatever we needed to start a new life.

Dick was out riding all day and, since there would be few opportunities for me to ride, I had time to explore this new country and practice cooking. I still wasn't the greatest cook, but I was trying. My mother-in-law was a fabulous cook and I wanted to do as well.

In my awkward way I chopped wood every day, manzanita wood, dry and brittle. I only succeeded in having enough to get by. Dick said I would probably cut my hand off or maim myself in some way, but I assured him I knew what I was doing. I wasn't really sure, but wouldn't admit it.

On Sundays, when Dick wasn't out riding, he would chop a big pile of wood. I still stubbornly chopped away at getting as much ready to use as possible. I didn't want him to say he had to do all the chores besides putting in a long day riding.

While we were living in Knights Ferry, the foreman's wife was taking lessons in leather carving. She agreed to teach me if I would buy the basic tools. I did. Before we left in June, I had made a lovely hand-tooled purse for my mother-in-law. It had a silver concho for a clasp. I was very proud of myself and decided to continue with the craft.

I liked to make pies and cookies and kept complaining about not having a rolling pin. I used an empty whiskey bottle that had been left in the flour bin by previous tenants. It worked, but not as well, so Dick decided to make me one out of redwood. It was the finest rolling pin I had ever seen, and I had it for years. When I could have had the most expensive one on the market, I still used my redwood rolling pin. I gave it away when I knew I wouldn't be needing one again. Now I wish I had kept it, as it was a real treasure.

The RO Ranch at Knights Ferry was owned by the Greene Cattle Company. (Photo donated by R. Blasingame)

Once in a while, on a Sunday, Dick would saddle up one of his horses for me and we would ride out and look over the cattle, especially if the weather brought an exceptionally fine day. Then, on some early evenings, if his day had been shorter than usual, we would take a .22 rifle and go bullfrog hunting along a branch of the Stanislaus River. I thought this was a lot of fun until I learned I was to be the retriever. It seemed as though, I ended up doing the most unpleasant jobs and being the pack mule in all our endeavors. Always there was a good reason why Dick couldn't do it. At least he cut off the frog's hind legs.

On one of these hunting expeditions he thought he had missed the first frog as it jumped into the water and sank

to the bottom of the stream. We continued following along the bank, looking for another one. On our way back to where we had started, lo and behold, there was one of the frogs, just coming out from the deep water. Then we noticed that the other three Dick had thought he'd missed were also on land. They were dead all right. Evidently come out on dry land even when they are shot between the eyes. A weird and scary sight.

Frog legs are good eating, and don't jump out of the pan when you fry them, like some people say. They wiggle and quiver while they are cooking, but you just have to remember how good they are going to taste. Nowhere else did we ever come across a place where we could hunt frogs.

The time in Knights Ferry was happy. When it came Christmastime, we decided we should have a bottle of cheer to celebrate our good fortune at finding such a wonderful job. With the help of friends, of course. So we went to Knights Ferry and in the liquor store bought a bottle of Frisky Mule. It was the cheapest bottle on the shelves, $1.75. We took it home and planned on having a nice hot toddy.

Well, we tried to drink our hot toddy, but neither of us could, no matter how much sugar we put in it. That bottle of Frisky Mule stayed with us until 1952 when Harve Rush, the sheep ranch hand, said there wasn't a brand of whiskey he couldn't drink. He was right because he drank it. He said it tasted awful but he'd drink it anyway. We kept the empty bottle for a keepsake for a long time. It finally fell off the shelf onto a cement floor and broke. So much for the Frisky Mule, aged at least six months.

When June came and the weather warmed up, Dick got itchy feet and kept talking about going back to New Meadows. I knew the wonderful job he had in Knights Ferry with the RO Cattle Company was coming to an end.

I hated to leave because it was such an exciting place to live.

But leave we did. We took the things we had bought, like the furniture, back to the second-hand store. The things we wanted to keep, we shipped to New Meadows. We were back to our one suitcase, his saddle and tack.

When he got his check, we hitchhiked to Winnemucca, then bussed the rest of the way into New Meadows. That was Dick's way of saving money. I'd sit on the side of the road on the suitcase and when a car came along I'd stand up and put out my thumb. Dick was lying on the ground so no one could see him. Some cars stopped and picked us both up, but often guys alone in a car drove off as soon as Dick stood up. It was a lot of fun then, but I sure wouldn't want to do it again.

Ike and Clara in Coarsegold wrote to us so we kept in touch. In one letter Clara wrote she had finally found out what a jigger of whiskey was. According to doctor's orders, her husband, Ike, was to have a jigger of whiskey once a day. Since Clara didn't drink and had never been in a barroom, she wasn't acquainted with the different kinds of glasses. She asked Ike what a jigger was. He went to the cupboard and took out a four-ounce juice glass.

"This is it," he said.

Clara gave him his four-ounce jigger but became curious as to why the bottles went so fast. On a trip to town to get more whiskey, Clara got up enough courage to enter the barroom and ask the bartender what a jigger was. He looked at her strangely but took one from the back bar to show her. Was she ever surprised!

She bought the glass right then and there. When she served Ike his whisky that night, he complained. She told him what she'd done and that was the end of Ike's big drink. So, you see, there were others learning things in life, too.

LARRY GARNER

There wasn't much work available in New Meadows but Dick got a job piling lumber into railroad cars. We lived on his folks' place in a one-room cabin. His dad still worked for the Circle C, but his mother was now cooking in one of the cafes in New Meadows. I got a job as a waitress in the same cafe. I worked an eight hour shift in that cafe, walked down the street a block, and put in a shift at another cafe. It was tough, but we needed the money to buy a car.

In the fall Dick was going to pack hunters for Larry Garner again in the Idaho Primitive Area. This time I was going along. We met Larry at New Meadows, then took off for the back country and Larry's base camp. This was at the end of the road. Cold Meadows and Chamberlain Basin were further on into the wilderness and accessed by trail.

The first thing to do was set up the camps for hunters. These were called spike camps. Our campsite was at the edge of a meadow, trees surrounding the area. To get ready for the hunters we cut wood and carried water, set up tents, outhouses, and meat poles, and took care of the stock. I was getting a different kind of education. This was the first time I'd lived in a tent.

Dick hobbled the bell mare and let the mules run loose. They wouldn't leave her. We took turns wrangling each morning. If he wrangled, I cooked breakfast and if I wrangled, he cooked. Sometimes the stock wandered a good distance away. I was a better rider now, since I rode almost every day. One morning, when it was my turn to wrangle, I had a hard time finding the stock. I didn't hear the bell for a long time. I was getting scared as I had to go farther than I ever had before. When I was about to give up, I heard the bell. It was easy to catch the mare, as I always carried a nosebag of oats. After I had her caught, I took the hobbles off and tied the bell clapper before heading for camp.

Everything went smoothly until something spooked the horses. The mare drew back. I lost the lead rope and the horse I was riding decided she was going to camp. I managed to keep her along the edge of the meadow; a creek zigzagged through the meadow and I had no desire to jump any creek. The mules went one way and I another. My horse was running her best, and I was hanging on for dear life. Then, all of a sudden, she stopped so quickly I almost went off over her head. Dick came out of the tent wondering what all the noise was about. That was the end of my riding that day. After breakfast Dick went after the stock. They were harder to find since he had no bell to follow.

One time, as we led the pack string across a meadow towards the timber, Dick looked up ahead and saw a deer. He said, "I'll go ahead and get some camp meat," and handed me the lead rope. He told me to walk my horse slowly, but not stop. Then he rode on ahead, jumped off his horse, and fired at the deer. What he hadn't counted on was the echo from the shot. It scared his horse, which turned and ran toward me.

The pack string went crazy. When they finally settled down, I was pinned on my horse with lead ropes every which way. How I got so tangled I will never know.

Dick said, "Don't move."

56

He caught his horse then came and started untying lead ropes to get the pack string untangled. What a mess. Worse yet, he missed the deer.

After the camps were set up and the first of the hunters taken care of, Larry asked us if we would finish out the season at his camp on Big Creek. So we packed, saddled up, and took off for a new camp. It was at Jess Taylor's place where Pioneer Creek runs into Big Creek, about twenty-five miles downstream from the town of Big Creek. We had a house all to ourselves on the opposite side of the creek from Jess and his wife, Dorothy. I remember having five members of the Cincinnati Reds baseball team on a hunt.

It was at Pioneer Creek that I first saw a coat made of bobcat pelts. Dorothy Taylor had one. Jess had trapped the cats and they had the hides made into a jacket in Boise. I thought how great it would be to have one, but Dick wasn't interested. Still, I thought about it a lot while at the Taylor place. After we left there, I forgot about it.

One thing I did often while we were there was cross Big Creek and go down the trail to an Indian campground. I'd spend a whole afternoon there. It was a fascinating place. I found lots of arrowheads, old army shells, and other bits of odds and ends. Several tepee holes were very visible.

Taylor Ranch was also the place where I had my first airplane ride. As the end of the season approached, Dick decided I should fly out. We radioed McCall to have Bob Fogg, when he could, take me out with him when he brought the mail.

I was really scared since I had never flown before. I waited and waited, and finally the week came. Mail day was on a Tuesday, I think, but whatever day it was, I was sure dreading it. I got on the plane and after we were in the air, Bob asked me if I'd like a cigarette. I took one, and then he began showing me places on the ground where he knew we had been. It wasn't long until I forgot I was flying and really enjoyed the trip.

After we landed at McCall, Bob told me he had made several trips to the area since he'd learned I was going out. Because it was my first flight, he chose this particular day. It was very calm. He said he liked to give a person the best flight possible the first time so the fear of flying would be lessened. I guess it worked that way with me because

Dick and Bonnie with bear rug. The bear was taken while Dick was working for Larry Garner. The rug was stored until the house was built and there was a place to use it.

I flew often after that.

Dick had a goat and a bear tag, so before he left Pioneer Creek for Cold Meadows he spent a few days hunting on his own. He was lucky in filling both tags. The goat horns were nine inches long. The bear, a big brown, measured 6 1/2 feet.

He packed the hides and heads back to Cold Meadows, brought them to New Meadows and took them to a taxidermist. He had a half-head-mount rug made of the bear and the goat head and neck mounted. It took several months. When they were finished we had them stored at his folks' place. At that time we had no place to use them.

The bear rug was beautiful. We found out, when we had a place to use it, that the half-head mount caused some problems. Unless you watched where you were going, it was easy to trip over. The goat skin was made into a rug, which later was mainly used for a wall hanging.

EUGENE, CALIFORNIA

After hunting season was over, we went to Boise and made a down payment on a car, our first. Returning to New Meadows, we loaded up our belongings and headed for California. Dick was expecting to get a job with the RO Ranch again, but they were filled for the winter. George Wiswal knew of a man who needed someone to halterbreak colts in Eugene, California, north of Oakdale. So we went to work for Mr. Ellenwood.

We had a big, rambling ranch house to live in, completely furnished. In earlier days it had been a stage stop. The big front room must have been the lobby. There was a big kitchen and pantry-laundry room, a dining room, and six bedrooms. A hallway ran down the middle of the house to the dining room. Doors on each side of the hallway opened into the bedrooms. Walnut, orange and lemon trees grew in the yard.

Across the road stood a big store with the post office. It looked as if people had just walked out and locked the door, leaving many early-day articles: canned goods, barrels, and even mail in the mail slots. It was a ghost store. There had been no business in that store for many, many years. The ranch house with its corrals and outbuildings and the store across the road were all the buildings in Eugene.

This was the place I thought Dick would stay. He was working with horses, doing the kind of work he enjoyed.

This was a grandiose place to live.

With Christmas approaching, I kept asking Dick to make a trip to Stockton. It was a little bigger town than Oakdale, and I wanted to see the Christmas decorations. That was one thing I missed about the little towns in the West. I was used to magnificent decorations in all the big stores back East. Finally, one evening after supper, he agreed to go. Before we had gone very many miles it began to show signs of being a very foggy night.

By the time we arrived in Stockton, the fog was so thick you could hardly see your hand in front of your face. Dick was growling all this time. Why did I have to come here? I wanted to shop around the stores, just looking. But Dick hated window shopping. I finally bought a nice, big, red candle.

When we started for home he said, "Since you wanted to go so bad, you drive home." That was one miserable ride. I could barely see the fog line on the edge of the road. He complained for months about my shopping trip in the fog, just for one candle.

When Christmas Eve came, we went to Oakdale. We decided to buy a Christmas tree. The prices were high. We looked everywhere they had trees for sale and finally came to a place that had only one tree left. It was a small cedar and no one wanted it. Since it was offered cheap, we bought it. We also bought some lights and a few ornaments, and drove home to decorate our first Christmas tree. It looked mighty festive when it was finally decorated and the lights turned on.

Once a month we'd go to Oakdale for groceries, doctor appointments, or just to go to town. After we'd finish up all the necessary errands and appointments, we'd just treat ourselves to a glass of beer before going back to the ranch. After ordering a beer, I'd pull out my Bull Durham sack and roll a smoke. Both Dick and I smoked and it was cheaper to smoke Bull Durham than store-bought "tailor-made" cigarettes. We used wheatstraw papers.

Soon one of the patrons at the bar would come over and ask me to roll another smoke. I guess not too many women rolled their own cigarettes then, but lots of people used machines, a small gadget for rolling cigarettes. I was always glad to roll someone a cigarette. Then Dick would say I could roll a cigarette with one hand. My father-in-law, Joe, had only one hand and he had taught me how. It was easy. The next thing I knew I had an audience. Before we left for home, all those in the bar who smoked were smoking cigarettes I'd rolled with one hand. Dick never bothered to show off and he didn't care about the one-handed bit. But for once, I was the one people noticed and talked to. I thought at the time I was pretty smart. We had a hired man living with us who did the regular ranch chores. I realized, as time went on, that he talked constantly of the wonders of Grand Canyon. He had worked at the canyon before coming to Eugene. I kept wishing he would keep quiet because I didn't want Dick to get it into his head to start traveling again. We had everything anyone could want right there.   By   the end of March Dick had been completely convinced that he was going to Grand Canyon. Then his folks came down from New Meadows for a visit. Since his folks had never been to San Francisco, we decided to take a couple of days and go see the big city.

We planned on staying overnight and seeing some of the sights. We weren't there long before we noticed we were on a one way street going the wrong way. We kept looking for a place to turn around. Before we could find a safe place, the cops stopped us.

The one who came to the car was very rough. When we asked him how we could get straightened out he yelled at us in a very rude manner. "I don't care how you do it, just get out of here."

We still had an Idaho license on the car so he could see we were from out of state, but that didn't mellow him any. We finally got turned around and headed out of town. So much for the big city. Back in Eugene, we decided we'd had plenty of the attitude of California police.

We had purchased a two-wheel trailer to haul the stuff we had acquired along the way. When we left Eugene for good we had eight gallons of shelled walnuts with us. There had been so many we hadn't made a dent in the crop. We enjoyed them for several years.

Grand Canyon

We arrived at Grand Canyon and what a sight! Snow was everywhere; it was still April and very cold. The snow outlined the jagged points of the canyon and contrasted against the reds, purples, and yellows of the rocks. Spring would be a few weeks away in this place.

I half forgot my sadness at leaving Eugene. Dick asked about a job with the U.S. Park Service. They told him we were too early. Come back in three weeks and we'd be hired. So we continued to travel around Arizona and enjoy the Petrified Forest National Park, the Painted Desert, and other sights of this new state.

When we returned to Williams, which is 60 miles from the park headquarters, we got a motel room and Dick's folks went back to New Meadows. We called Grand Canyon headquarters and told them where we were staying. Then we inquired in Williams for any work available. The motel owner told me I could get a job as a waitress in the only cafe, but there was no work for Dick. I worked until the day they called from the park.

The Park Service

For a few days we stayed in a Park Service cabin and then were taken to Indian Gardens Camp Ground, six miles down the Bright Angel Trail. Dick was to maintain the trails.

Our cabin was near the campground. It had big rock corners on the outside, a kitchen, bedroom, and bath. It was small but neat and comfortable and close to the main trail where the dude strings came down. A barn and corrals were located above the house next to the rock bluff.

We were told to be sure and hang up our clothes, shake them vigorously before putting them on, and never put our hands in a drawer or cupboard without looking first. The bed legs were set in one pound coffee cans of stove oil to keep the scorpions from crawling up on the bed. There was nothing to keep them from falling off the ceiling, though none ever did. We were never bitten but I can tell you I was very careful.

We had a good time at Indian Gardens. We met people at the campground and got acquainted with all the guides. Weekends we explored the canyon beyond the main trail. Dick rode a mule and I rode the only horse in the canyon, a black mare called Blacky.

Each time we rode to Grand Canyon Village on the rim, Dick would spend his time in the barn with the Fred Harvey guides. The Fred Harvey Guide Service, supplying mule rides for tourists into the canyon, had headquarters at the village. While Dick visited, I would go to the store and post office and then we'd pack our supplies back into the canyon.

By now I had nearly forgiven Dick for leaving Eugene. Grand Canyon and our life there was really a wonder of wonders. There was so much to do and see. When the last dude string had left the canyon for the day, it became a quiet, peaceful place. We could sit and watch the lizards climb around in our cactus garden.

Some nights when we wanted some excitement we'd each get a broom. Dick would go out on the porch. I'd turn the lights out and after a bit turn them on and run out.

We'd bang away at the scorpions to see how many we could get. There were millions of them.

Along in August I had to go out to the hospital for surgery. While I was gone a cloudburst hit the canyon. Dick had done a washing and hung it out. Most of it went down the Colorado along with the government tent and all our stored belongings. The cloudburst made a waterfall through our bathroom window and right out the front door. What a mess.

It had only lasted a few minutes, but it left a foot or better of mud and silt in the house. Now I knew the reason for the big rock corners of the house: to keep it anchored during flash floods. Most of the mess was cleaned up when I got back. A crew was sent in to repair the trail and I cooked for them. That way I made some extra money for myself.

During Dick's visits to the Fred Harvey barn he learned that a packing job for Fred Harvey was going to open up in September. This was more to his liking than trail maintenance, so he applied. Before long we loaded our belongings on a mule and moved out of the Canyon to work for Fred Harvey and live at Yaqui Point along the south rim.

YAQUI POINT

This move wasn't very far—six miles out of the canyon and four miles along the rim to Yaqui Point. As we turned off the main road, the corral and barn were on the left, the house where we lived on the right. At the head of the trail was the registration box and the Park Service house where their packer, Guy May, lived. The drive continued in a circle to the front of the barn.

Our house had four rooms, completely furnished, with an outhouse situated conveniently out the back door.

Electricity was provided by a generator. We had done very well by moving this time. The barn was huge with a runway through the center wide enough for trucks to drive in and unload hay, grain, salt, and all the supplies for Phantom Ranch. Stalls for the mules lined one side of the runway and a loading platform the other. A room at the end of this platform stored the grain and salt. The scale for weighing packs was the kind you had to put a penny in. Pennies were not furnished.

Mule Barn At Grand Canyon Village. The blacksmith shop was also in this barn where the mules were kept. Guides lived in cabins nearby and took tourists into the canyon on mules. A one-day trip was to Indian Gardens, a two-day trip was to Phantom Ranch with accommodations at the ranch. (Photo donated by Ron Clayton)

This was a dream job. I had never heard of one like it before, nor have I since. All our groceries were furnished. We just went to Babbitt's Store in the village, wrote in a special book each item we bought and the price. Everything was allowed except cigarettes, beer, and clothes. All gas, tires, and repairs were furnished for the car.

Not only were our gas and groceries furnished, all our laundry, except personal clothing, was done at the laundry and returned to the barn. All I had to do was take the dirty linens, towels, bedspreads, and tablecloths to the hamper in the barn and get clean ironed ones. This really was the life of Riley. I figured we would be here a long time and save a stake for the future. But my thoughts and Dick's seldom matched.

Front View of Barn at Yaqui. The door on this barn was large enough for trucks to drive through. (Photo donated by Ron Clayton)

The only pack saddles we had to work with were sawbucks, the kind used mainly in the South. Dick, coming from the North, had learned to pack with the Decker saddle. He decided to buy his own saddles. No one had heard of Deckers, let alone stocked them, so he ordered eight to be made. I remember it took six weeks to make them. Meanwhile Dick had to use the sawbucks.

Barn At Yaqui Point. Local rock was used to build this huge barn where all the salt, grain, laundry, hay, and supplies were kept ready to be packed into Phantom Ranch. All cargoeing was done on the platforms and packs arranged in proper order for loading. (Photo donated by Ron Clayton)

Making these saddles was a new experience for the saddlemaker. No one around the Canyon had heard of such a saddle and there was a lot of speculation as to the outcome. When the saddles finally arrived and each was fitted to a mule and ready to go, everyone in Grand Canyon Village was there to watch. They all said the saddles wouldn't work. Absolutely wouldn't! The first morning down the trail, John Bradley, the mule boss, went along. He was amazed at how good they were. That ended the doubts about the Decker.

Not long after we started this job a new foreman for the

Side View Of The Barn At Yaqui Point. (Photo donated by Ron Clayton)

Park Service, Bill Yenne, arrived. Coming from Montana, he was also a Decker saddle man. He and Dick hit it off real well and his wife Doris and I became fast friends. The Park Service changed to Deckers as soon as Bill arrived and continued with them. When we left the canyon we took our saddles with us and the new Fred Harvey packer went back to the sawbucks. Later, they returned to Decker saddles, according to Ron Clayton, the packer employed at the time of this writing.

We took a full string, eight head, down the trail into the canyon. Every pack going down the canyon, whether it was laundry, groceries, hay, grain, salt, or whatever, had to be cargoed the same width. The trail was four feet wide all the way. The Kaibab Suspension Bridge over the Colorado River and the tunnels at each end were only five feet wide. Hay bales would rub each side of the bridge and, as many times as the mules had crossed the bridge, at least one of them would spook and try to cause some kind of fracas while crossing the suspension bridge. I had some misgivings a few times at first. It was 500 feet down

New sign at the head of the Kaibab Trail. This is the trail we went down every day. We called this trail "The Yaqui Trail" because we were living on Yaqui Point. (Photo taken by Ron Clayton)

to the river. Took some getting used to.

Life became routine: up by 4 a.m., down the trail by 5:30 a.m., back to the barn by 1 or 2 p.m., packs off, mules cared for, and packs cargoed for the next day. A blacksmith in the village, Frank Bradney, shod all the mules.

It was a wonderful life. After the packs were cargoed, the rest of the day was free. This was such a beautiful place to live. The sunsets were gorgeous, never the same. The storms thrilled me. Sometimes they were scary but still exciting, and I loved them.

On the road from the village to Yaqui Point was a sign reading "Tarantula Crossing." At certain times of the day, armies of tarantulas crossed the road. They came out of the canyon at night and returned in the morning. Or was it the other way around? Can't remember for sure, but some people in the village would try to see how big a tarantula they could find. The biggest one I ever saw filled a one-pound coffee can, the flat, squatty kind that coffee used to come in.

It was at Yaqui Point that I resumed my riding lessons and rode every day. We rode mules all the time; there were no horses. I had three special saddle mules, June, Dot and Les. Each gave me trouble at one time or another, all caused by my own carelessness. I had no one to blame but myself

Here, also, I decided to learn how to pack. I'd come a long way from when I couldn't even saddle or mount my horse by myself. The first thing to learn was how to cargo. Dick had me start on laundry since it was easier. When I could tie up a decent pack I practiced on bales of hay. They each weighed 75 pounds. I only weighed 95 at the most, so it took quite a while before I could lift a bale of hay, carry it over to the mule, and tie it on. I practiced every day until I mastered it. For once in my life, I had really accomplished something. From that time on until we left the canyon I did my share of cargoing and packing. It was easy to become careless riding the trail every day, and I did my share of that. Dick kept saying that as soon as I got my new saddle, there wasn't a mule that could buck me off. How dumb I was to believe him.

The following spring Dick made out an order for my Garcia saddle. It was going to be just for me, with silver conchos and the works. It would be fully stamped in a wild rose pattern with my name on the back of the 3-inch cantle. The weeks went by. As it came closer to the time the new saddle would arrive, I couldn't get out of the canyon fast enough to do up our work and drive into the village to the post office to see if it was there.

When it did arrive, Dick got to the post office before I did, picked up the saddle and rushed home with it. He took it out of the box, caught my mule, and fitted it to him.

When I came home, there it was on the mule.

I was hurt and furious! I couldn't believe my eyes. How could he have done such a thing to me? His folks were visiting at the time so I had to hide my feelings, but the fact that he hadn't let me open the box and take the saddle out was really painful. It robbed me of the thrill of being the first to see this beautifully-crafted leather and silver masterpiece. After all, it was mine. He told me later he had gone for a ride on my mule first also. So even though I loved my saddle very much, there was also the sadness from the day it arrived. I still feel the same way today and I guess I always will.

Once, as we came out of the canyon on a hot day, I was sitting half in the saddle and half out, if you know what I mean, one foot out of the stirrup, off to one side.

I decided to roll a smoke. I very seldom smoked on the trail. Why I did that day I'll never know. I wrapped the reins around the saddle horn, another thing I was told never to do, and got the cigarette rolled. As I reached in my pocket for a match, the mule jumped.

Of course I tried to reach for the reins but it was too late. I'd lost my balance. I fell over backwards and hung with one foot in the stirrup. There I hung while Les, the mule, ran up the trail, my head at his heels. Dick was behind with the pack string and couldn't do a thing but watch. Fortunately, I was sure the mule wouldn't kick because they were broke not to, and he didn't.

I hung there. When I couldn't see anything but air over the edge of the trail, I hung quietly. When I could see trees or brush I kicked like fury trying to get loose. I finally did and fell in the middle of the trail.

Dick came up from behind. As he got off his mule the first thing he said was, "For a while there, I thought I was going to have to get a new wife."

I can tell you I was mad then. I was mad at him, at the

mule, and mad at myself because it was all my fault. I had done everything Dick had told me never to do.

My mule went clear to the barn without me, so Dick put me on his mule while he walked to the top. I never did anything like that again. Once was enough. If I hadn't hung in the stirrup when the mule jumped, as off balance as I was, I would have fallen off the trail into space. So I was saved that time to make a stupid mistake another day. It seems like I was prone to be doing things I knew I shouldn't do.

Another time, as we came out of the canyon, I had an unfortunate accident at the registration box, the place where people who walked into the canyon signed their names, indicated where they were going and when they planned to be back. If they didn't show up at the right

A Switchback on the Yaqui Trail. Fred Harvey packers took supplies into the canyon to the Phantom Ranch daily and brought laundry and miscellaneous items out. (Photo donated by Ron Clayton)

A Typical 8-mule Pack String. Bonnie is watching the rear of the string. Lead mule Spider is ground-tied to keep him out of trouble.

Bonnie and Pack String On Yaqui Trail. The Yaqui Trail was four feet wide, wide enough so a packed mule would not brush against rock or bridge railings.

Bonnie Leading a Pack String. Grand Canyon formations make a spectacular backdrop for packers as they travel daily to Phantom Ranch.

time, someone could go look for them. I had seen this box at the head of the trail every day. At this particular time someone left the book on top and the wind was fluttering the pages. When I got even with the box, I leaned way out of the saddle to look at the book. At the same time my mule jumped, leaving me sitting on the ground. With a new saddle no mule could buck me off? Again it was my fault, and why I did it I'll never know. The only thing I could think of was whether any of the people who came out to watch the pack string come up out of the canyon had seen me. I was lucky this day as there was no one around. My mule only went a couple of steps and stopped. I got on him and made a mad dash for the barn.

Again I was mad at myself for doing such a dumb thing and Dick laughed all the way to the barn. Of course everyone in the canyon knew about it within twenty-four hours because Dick thought it was so funny he had to tell the world. It's not even funny today. No wonder Dick kept saying to me, "How can you live so long and be so dumb?" It was easy I guess. It seems I was always struggling to do the right thing and ending up getting into some kind of mess.

In winter we had a different schedule. When the Yaqui trail snowed in we went down the Bright Angel Trail, stayed overnight at the Phantom Ranch, and returned the next day. Spare time was used braiding rope and making halters, lead ropes, cargo ropes, and pigtails.

Bonnie on the Bright Angel Trail in Winter. Others in the photo are Dick, other friends, and Bill Yenne leading the Park Service string. The Bright Angel Trail was kept open during the winter.

Pigtails were small quarter-inch ropes looped at both ends. They were used to string out the mules by fastening one end to the pack saddle and tying the lead rope of the next mule to the other end.

Indian Gardens Campground. A lunch break on Bright Angel Trail includes both Park Service and Fred Harvey Pack Service mule strings, two 8-mule strings.

The first winter got real cold. I couldn't buy overshoes small enough to fit my boots, so Dick wrapped them in gunny sacks. It was better than nothing. Awkward at times, but it worked.

As for social activities in the park there were no bars unless there was one at the El Tovar Hotel. I don't know as I was never in there. Occasionally, during the summer, informal jackpot rodeos were held just outside the park.

For a few weeks the following summer I worked at Verkamp's in the village. They sold beautiful Indian jewelry, pottery, rugs, blankets, and petrified wood like I'd never seen. I enjoyed the job, but before long the mules, trails and packing became more important, so I quit and went back to riding every day.

Bonnie at Verkamps Curio Store. Bonnie worked at this Grand Canyon Village store. The Indian items were from the store. (Photo by Mabel Everly)

The small, wild burros in the canyon were a nuisance. At times the mules in the string were curious and had to be watched very carefully so they didn't get mixed up and cause an accident. The Park Service had a couple of burro roundups while we were there. I always wished I could have a burro, but I wouldn't have been able to keep it.

Our lead mule, Spider, was big and black. He had to be watched at all times. He was just a bad mule. Sometimes a mule in the pack string was one that had bucked off a dude or a guide. Most of the time, after a dude mule was packed for awhile he was okay for the dude string again.

While we were there we decided to take a couple days off and ride across the canyon to the North Rim. We took the usual loaded pack string down to Phantom Ranch and left the mules in the corral. We stayed overnight at Cottonwood with the people who were working for the Park Service. Next morning we rode on to the North Rim. When we topped out at the head of the trail, there were several guides at the barn. They kept looking at me, and a lot of whispering was going on. They were all very friendly and, after a nice visit, we left to get back to the South Rim.

When we got down the trail a ways, Dick told me the reason the fellows were whispering. It was because I was riding a mule that had bucked them all off and had been turned over to the packer. I was dumped by almost every mule I rode, but it was because of something I did rather than the mule wanting to buck. Other than the stupid things I did, I never had any trouble with my saddle mules.

What with riding every day and learning to pack, life was simply great. This was such a beautiful place to live and, even though it was a National Park, we were not associated with the visitors there.

Occasionally I stayed overnight at Phantom Ranch because the people there, Gene and Ida Connor and Emma Poquet, were very accommodating and friendly. Gene was the chef and a good one. All this made it fun to stay overnight. Of course, the only time I could was when they had a vacant cabin.

We very seldom went to Williams as there really wasn't much to go for. Once, when we were coming back from Williams, just about dusk, we saw there were a lot of deer in the area. Many deer ate with the mules at night. They weren't exactly pets, but they weren't afraid of you either. Noticing a few along the edge of the road, I decided I'd better stop and see what they had in mind. They just stood there and looked at me. I started to move along and so did they. Then about seven of them jumped on the hood of the car. Talk about a bent hood! I drove the car into the garage in town the next morning and in a few days it was fixed as good as new.

Every thing was running smoothly. At times I wondered how long this idyllic life would last. Dick's folks came for a visit and decided to work a few weeks at Phantom Ranch. They soon left again for Idaho. After they left, Dick began to talk more of Idaho than Arizona. I knew sooner or later he was going to give up this job and head north. By now I knew that all good things come to an end, but I sure did hate the thought of leaving Grand Canyon. I knew we would never have such a job again. I guess you have to do what you think is right at the time and it wasn't long before we were packing our two-wheel trailer again and heading north.

PAISLEY

Instead of going to Idaho, we stopped off at Paisley, Oregon, where Dick and I met. Dick went to work again at the ZX. Before long I found myself also working for the ZX. I cooked at the Red House where Dick was staying, ten miles northeast of Paisley. This is when I learned to cook for more than one or two people. Forty men actually. Eighteen cowboys and twenty-two ranch hands were at the table. I wrote to Betty Crocker and she sent me recipes for making cakes and cookies, pie fillings, and all kinds of things. Everything started from scratch. All vegetables were peeled; none came from cans. It didn't take much of that work for me to wish I was somewhere else.

We had the same thing to eat every morning for breakfast: steak, baking powder biscuits with gravy, and coffee. Always steak. They butchered a yearling beef every week. I got up very early in the morning and started frying the steak. As I fried the steak I put it in a big roasting pan. When all were brown they went into the oven of this huge, wood stove. Mrs. Johnson, my boss, made the biscuits and gravy. I set the table and lighted the kerosene lamps in the dining area. It was a rush every morning to have the meal ready on time. While the men were eating I started making lunches for the few ranchhands and the cowboys who asked for one. They didn't ask very often.

Keeping the big kitchen and dining area clean was a huge chore. I also filled the lamps and washed the chimneys. I was inexperienced in most of this work, but what I learned came in handy later.

The cowboys went out before daylight to rope horses for the day's ride. They wrangled the horses into a single-rope corral held up by several cowhands. On the morning I left I went out and watched them rope, amazed at how they could pick out their horses just by the shape of the ears or the head.

Dick would come back in the middle of the afternoon and take off with the single buckaroos while I had supper to cook. So I was stuck.

That didn't set very well. Before long I'd had enough. When I quit, Dick quit too. We pulled out for New Meadows, Idaho, to spend Christmas with his folks.

So this ended another episode in our lives. I knew we would be starting on a new way of life but had no idea of what was to come.

A Home at Slate Creek

On the way to Idaho we talked about finding a place to winter on the Salmon River. We intended to head south again come spring. While we were in New Meadows for the holidays, we made several trips to Salmon River, Riggins, Slate Creek and White Bird. Dick wasn't looking for a job. We were looking for a place to camp. In New Meadows, it was 35 degrees below zero or colder with lots of snow. We wanted a warmer climate and these places down the Salmon toward White Bird were lower altitude and definitely milder.

We met and talked with people who lived along the river and learned that camping just anywhere was impossible. In our inquiries we were told that Bill and Mamie Robie, who lived near the mouth of Slate Creek on the Salmon River, would be our best bet. We stopped at their ranch. They had some land up the creek they were thinking of selling. Since we weren't having any luck renting a place, Dick decided we'd better do a little more thinking about it. We told the Robies we'd be back after Christmas. Since Dick did all the deciding, I just listened. His theory was we could buy the place, have somewhere to camp all winter, and just pack up and leave when spring came. Since there were no buildings on the land, we'd have no worries about leaving it.

Now I was getting interested in what was maybe going to take place. But from past experience I knew better than to say anything and just agreed to whatever was decided. After Christmas we drove back to Slate Creek. Meanwhile Robies had decided they would sell their land and Dick had decided it was a good investment.

About ten acres of flat land lay along the creek and about twenty-three acres or so was rocky hillside. A fence separated the property from Mahurin's on the west and Chandler's on the east. Lots of trees and brush lined the creek. Above the road, a fence divided the rocky hillside between Chandler's on the east and Large's on the west. A ditch ran the full length of the hillside, separating us on the north from Large's. The flat was fenced in and about midway along the road was a wire gate. Probably the land had been used for pasture.

We set a date to meet with the Robies in Grangeville to complete the deal. On the ride back to New Meadows the talk was all about what we would need to spend the winter at Slate Creek. It was January, 1950. We met the Robies in Grangeville at the appointed time. It was a cold, stormy day but since this was a new venture in our life we didn't mind a bit.

After all the business was completed, we noticed that the weather was changing. Snow was starting to fall. The Robies advised us to stay in town overnight. It was snowing hard on White Bird Hill.

The next morning, after a leisurely breakfast, we headed out of town. Snow still fell. By the time we got to the foothills we saw car after car lined up. The road was blocked with snow. The plow finally came by and the driver told us to turn around and go back to town. There was no way we could get through that day.

The next morning we started a little earlier. It was still storming and again we had to go back to town. This was something we hadn't planned on. On the third morning we got up very early. The snow had stopped falling but the wind still blew. We were lucky enough to get through.

When we reached Slate Creek we stopped to see the Robies. They had come through the previous day before snow closed the newly-opened road. We learned not to linger in town if it was storming on White Bird Hill.

We drove back up the creek and again looked over our land. No buildings had been built, and I thought there was a possibility of having a nice home here. We returned to New Meadows knowing there were lots of things to do.

Next day we drove seventy-seven miles to Weiser to purchase supplies. We bought a green, waterproof army tent, 12 by 14 feet with 5-foot side walls. Also a nice cookstove, about 24 by 17 inches standing on 8-inch high legs. It turned out to be the best little cook stove you could possibly imagine. Just right for a tent. By the time we had our necessary purchases and returned to New Meadows, it was late in the day.

The next day we were loading our two-wheel trailer with all our belongings. Dick's folks supplied us with lots of odds and ends they weren't using. We were getting short of cash so we were grateful for all the things they gave us.

It was about fifty-six miles from New Meadows to Slate Creek and it was afternoon when we got there. We had stopped to have our supper in Riggins at Summerville's, a restaurant and bar, since we had nothing set up to cook with. Dick cut tent poles and we stretched up the tent and staked it down just enough to get through the night. It was much warmer and pleasant along the creek after the cold in New Meadows.

We rolled out our sleeping bags on a feather bed his folks had given us and called it a day. During the night the wind came up, blowing the tent down over us. That woke us up in a hurry. The tent was very heavy, but Dick scrambled out somehow, found a cargo rope and tied the ridge pole to a birch tree near by. We had set the tent by the birch tree for shade later on. It came in handy then. Somehow we managed to get back to sleep.

By morning the wind had died down, but we knew how hard it could blow. We would need to have a more substantial shelter than just the staked tent. Dick decided to get some lumber and build a tent frame.

We drove to Riggins for breakfast and then got what was needed at the mill. Back at Slate Creek we unloaded our supplies. Dick knew just how to build a frame, putting down stringers and then flooring. Uprights were added and tied together with 2 x 4s to make a solid frame. To this he nailed the rafters, one set at each end with a ridge pole. The pitch of the roof was determined by the tent. He then put 1 x 12 boards three feet up on the sides. It was quite a job for one day, with meals cooked over a campfire.

The next day we stretched the tent over the frame. The five-foot side walls on the tent were pulled down over the 1 x 12s until the tent fit the frame. The walls were five and a half feet and the peak at the ridge pole less than eight feet. The tent would be easy to heat and we didn't need more height. Dick had bought this special tent with these measurements in mind. It fit like a glove and was nailed down to the frame using lath to keep it from flapping. There was very little movement.

The stove was set up so the pipe, which was on the right side of the stove, came at the first seam. It fit in just right. We moved in and had our first real meal in our new tent house, our home for the next two years. In time Dick built shelves on each side of the doorway for dishes and a small shelf for the water bucket. Then he put in two solid-pane glass windows, one between the first and second seam on the east and the other between the end of tent and the first seam on the west. The Coleman lantern hung from the center of the ridge pole. If you didn't look up you could

By Eugene Hayes ©
5·9·95

Approximate sketch of the tent house we lived in for two years. (Drawn by Eugene Hayes)

almost believe that you were living in a one-room house. It was warm and cozy.

In spite of the warmer climate, the weather was cold and stormy. Ice began forming along the creek. It got harder every day to find a safe place to get a bucket of water. We used a lot of wood, but there was plenty to cut: alder, birch, cottonwood, chokecherry, seedling apple, elderberry, hackberry, and all kinds of brush that needed to be cleared. Dick knew he had to build an outhouse so he built a temporary one we could settle in quickly. It was better than none at all.

We were kept busy getting wood. The water bucket froze every night, but it didn't take long to warm things up after a fire was built. The tent house drew curious stares from those who drove up the creek. I don't imagine there had been too many tent houses built along here for quite some time, if ever.

A platform porch in front made it easier to enter the tent. Dick built a door from lath, some 1 x 6s, and some old canvas. We had bought a congoleum rug for the floor and acquired a bedspring and mattress. A small closet at the back end held clothing. We acquired a work table, 18 1/2 by 27 inches that fit below the west window. Later, when we moved from the tent, I removed the legs and used the top for a bread board. It is still in use today, well-seasoned.

By the time we'd lived a month in the tent, we had things pretty comfortable. Thus, we became very warm and cozy in our home on Slate Creek even though it got below zero that January and February and every day we chopped ice in the frozen creek to get water.

In the evenings, pencil and paper emerged and talk of a log house was uppermost in Dick's mind. I didn't get too excited at that time because, after all, this was just a place to camp for the winter. And winter it was. But Dick talked less and less about where he wanted to go when spring came.

By the end of February the creek was frozen solid. We thawed chunks of ice and strained the water to drink. Then a Chinook wind came along and it wasn't long until the ice began to crack. Somewhere up the creek the ice came loose and huge chunks came down the creek. It made a terrific noise and, as we watched, ice chunks rolled end on end. Some landed out in the field. It was a sight to see. The creek cleared of ice and once again it flowed freely. I was getting used to the winds that came up or down the creek and loved the sound of the water. Some years later I would learn more about the power and destruction of water when it went on a rampage.

When the ice thrown up on land finally melted I picked up several trout still alive and freed of ice. I tossed them, not back into the creek, but into the skillet.

After the thaw, Dick diverted a small stream of water closer to the tent, making a waterfall. Then it was easier to get water. . .until it froze again.

After all necessary things were done, Dick built another door out of 1 x 8s with the traditional latch string. Later a screen door was added.

In March a storm put six inches of snow on the ground. It was beautiful. I took a walk the full length of the flat and marveled at the realization this all was ours. When it quit snowing the sun came out and by the next day the snow was gone.

With more and more talk of the possibilities of this place, Dick began to think of building some corrals. When the weather got warmer, he'd start breaking some horses. Then he decided the car we had was not adequate for the work ahead. He traded it for a little red army jeep. It was kinda' scary riding in it the first few times. Seemed like you were sitting pretty close to the road. As with everything else, I got used to this change.

When the ground thawed, Dick built two large, round, stockade-style corrals of yew wood. Since it was free for the taking, discarded telephone wire was used to fasten the wood together. With lumber, hinges and nails for gates, and plenty of back breaking work, he had his cost-free corrals.

When he started breaking horses and shoeing stock for people who needed it, I was to do my part also. It was never an easy task. I hadn't been on a horse since Grand Canyon.

We kept the horses in our pasture and Dick rode them for thirty days. I hated it when I had to ride one of his green-broke horses. They wouldn't buck, but they still

90

had a lot of training to go through before they would behave predictably.

I spent a good many hours a day helping Dick get started. It was a lot easier when two people worked together. I helped him catch, tie down, and hobble many a horse. One way I helped was by holding the horse's head down on the ground and covering it with a gunny sack. With my knee on its neck it couldn't throw its head or try to get up and hurt itself. That gave Dick an easier job putting on sack hobbles.

The only time I wasn't needed was when someone else stopped by, and then I was told to go to the tent. It didn't take long to figure out that the minute someone drove up, I was to get lost. There was always plenty of other work, which was a lot easier on me anyway.

Now that Dick was working with horses and had acquired some of his own, he purchased a used horse trailer. He knew he would be needing one.

My mother-in-law gave me a rod and reel, line, hooks, the works, for my birthday. She was going to teach me how to fish. She gave me all the basic instructions with a final word on the use of the reel. When you catch a fish, she said, use the reel to wind up the line. Never jerk the line out of the water. If you do, you are an "Arkansas fisherman."

Well, after all her training, I became the best darn Arkansas fisherman in Idaho. I could never remember I had a reel. I was always afraid I would lose the fish. Our two Manx cats went fishing with me every time I went. It was a mad scramble to see who got the fish first from somewhere in the field behind me. Or we'd all watch to see where it was going to land when the line caught high in a tree overhead. Most of the time the fish flipped off into the creek, but it was also exciting at times to see who was going to have fish for supper. I fished this way until I went to the Snake River and could not throw the sturgeon and catfish out onto the sand bar. But whenever I fished in the creeks I went back to the old way ninety percent of the time. Habits are hard to break.

That summer our friends, Clark and Beulah Cox, gave us a dozen Banty chickens. They had to do something with them since they were heading for the mountains for the summer. We had no place to keep chickens but they wanted us to have them anyway. We took them and just turned them loose. Predators got some, and, when we decided we'd better catch them before they were all gone, we had to use the .22 pistol to get them. They were just too wild to get anywhere near. We ended up with five of the dozen, so that wasn't too bad. Good thing the Coxes didn't want them back. They would have been disappointed.

One afternoon I took a lawn chair out to the east side of the tent to rest. I was just sitting there daydreaming when I heard the clucking of a quail. I sat real still since I didn't know where the sound was coming from for sure. Then I looked down and out from under my chair came the tiniest baby quail I had ever seen. As I counted, the covey came into sight and there were twenty-two. The mother hen was off to my right, busy as she could be trying to keep her family under control. What a sight! I had never before seen so many little ones. I sat there watching them and hoped our two Manx cats weren't around.

Not much was said about leaving for someplace else. The building of a log house was now the topic of conversation. More and more plans were drawn with dimensions and number of logs needed. Sketches of the flat and the exact place where it would be built appeared. Finally we decided on the spot and started marking off the foundation. Then Dick changed his mind and built near the birch tree. As he said, he would need all of the flat for his horses.

Things were going well. Dick was bringing in some money with his horse-breaking and the days were slipping by. Since he had made a decision to stay here a little longer, we began talking of raising a garden. Lots of wild blackcaps grew at the upper end of the property. Since it was a narrow strip of land we decided that would be a good garden plot.

Some people at Slate Creek planted early gardens in February, but not all years. Harry Parent was the first one at Slate Creek that year to raise an early garden, so he had the honor of having the first ripe tomato, the goal of all who raised a garden in this area.

We borrowed gardening equipment from Dick's folks, sent off for all sorts of seed, and prepared to stay the summer. I let my imagination run wild. Perhaps this was where we would settle down, and have no more packing up to go somewhere else. That summer we cut our logs at Lost Valley with a crosscut saw. The Forest Service marked the trees and they had to be cut at a certain number of inches from the ground. Then the logs were peeled and decked. We also had to pile the tops and limbs. That was extremely hard work, but enjoyable, as it was to be our home. Dick's uncle hauled the logs for us.

The building was 20 by 30 feet. When it came time to start building and putting up the logs, Dick borrowed a level, plumb bob, and chalk line from his folks. We owned the axe. That was a necessity, used every day.

Getting the logs up for the walls was difficult with what we had to work with. The peeled logs were slick and hard to handle. Using ropes and skids, we cross-hauled them into position. I did ninety percent of the driving of the jeep for the cross-haul and then Dick used a peavy to jockey them into place after he had made the notches. It was rough going after the logs got up to some height, impossible always to stop when he yelled. And yell he did with most of the words unprintable. If I didn't do just right he would get too mad to give me another chance. Then he would struggle furiously by himself and I'd take off for the safety of the tent. When tempers calmed, we'd start in all over again. What fond memories there are of building our dream house.

When he put uprights for the door and windows the logs settled and the ones on top bowed slightly. He was sure learning what not to do when cutting logs and starting to build.

When the weather got real hot Dick quit breaking horses. Since we had such a big garden, he decided we needed a cellar to store all the food I would put up. With a cooker canner, jars, and a Kerr canning book, I did learn to can. Everything edible in sight went into jars. All excess produce that summer was taken to New Meadows to Shaver's store and sold.

That summer a sawmill went in at Slate Creek. Dick went down and got some 2 x 4s and some shims. The shims were free for the taking. That was what Dick built our cellar out of. It had 12-inch walls filled with sawdust from the mill. The door was also a foot thick and filled with sawdust. It was heavy to open and close, but nothing ever froze inside. We bought nice planed lumber for shelves and inside walls. When we got electricity, it finally had a light in it, too. If I'm not mistaken, the cellar still stands today after forty years. There was never a time from when it was built until the day we moved that it was empty.

Our tent house was very comfortable. Our furniture consisted of the bed, two chairs, and a small kitchen table. Although the house logs were up, it still needed the rafters, the roof, floor and windows.

Dick decided to put up another tent frame so we would

have a bedroom. This tent was white, nine by twelve, nice and bright and cheery. After it was up and the floor put in, we moved the bed to that tent. Dick built another closet and we were given a small, used davenport and chair. We were getting things done in a big way.

Doing laundry was a chore. Water was packed from the waterfall Dick had created and heated in the round laundry tub on our little cook stove. Only the wash water was heated. Rinsing was in cold water. The washboard and I became about as good friends as you can get with something as hard to put up with as it was. Dick finally got around to stringing up a clothesline. No more hanging clothes on a cargo rope or on bushes. I used sadirons, heated on the stove, since we had no electricity. I did have a regular ironing board, though.

About this time a GI school started in the area. This was a program to help returned servicemen get a start in agriculture. Everett Chaney, who lived on the main Salmon River at Horseshoe Bend, was instructor. Each one in the class was to raise something for themselves. Most of them had cattle. We needed to decide what we could raise.

We decided to get a hundred chicks for our project. We would leave them in New Meadows with Dick's folks, who had a fenced chicken yard and a well-built chickenhouse. We figured if we bought the feed and supplies that would suffice as Dick's project. We didn't have facilities on our place for chickens, or anything else for that matter.

Things went along real well until someone got curious about not seeing any chickens at our place on the creek. Then Dick's mother was talking about how Dick had this project for the GI school and she was raising his chickens for him. It wasn't long before the word got to the school administrator and Dick was disqualified. It was fun while it lasted. We had to go to New Meadows and butcher all

95

the chickens. We put them in a freezer locker in Riggins.

We raised chickens together with his folks after that. It didn't take that many to keep us, as we always had lots of elk and venison. We also had fish from the creek, in season.

Before Dick was disqualified, he suggested to the that class they ought to build a log barn. Chaney agreed and a day was picked for the barnraising. Dick had cut some logs to build the barn himself but now he would have some help. The whole class showed up with their axes. Dick showed them how it was done. Chaney showed them how to cut rafters and put on sheathing and roofing. It was a pretty good barn for so many doing the chopping and it was completed in one day.

When that was done, Dick had Chaney come and help him put the rafters, sheathing, and roof on our cabin. Now we had a roof but no floor. These things take time and we had done so much in the few months we had been here.

GI school barn. Bonnie is shown with saddle horses.

Bonnie and Lynx rug. Bonnie is standing by the unfinished log house on Slate Creek. The GI barn can be seen through the two windows. The Lynx skin was given to Bonnie and Dick by Pick Ward.

We decided we would have a fireplace in our log house. We hired Army White of Riggins to come down and do the work. We used rock from the creek. I think the fireplace was about 8 feet wide, centered at one end of the cabin. We put in a heat-a-lator unit and two fans at the outlets. This was a beautiful addition to the cabin.

We now had two tent houses and a log cabin with roof and fireplace. We were coming along piece by piece. Next would be getting some windows ordered for the cabin and the subfloor put in. Dick would get the floor material from the sawmill at Slate Creek. It was a great convenience that the mill went in that summer.

We ordered some trees to plant that spring, five poplars for the west and two blue spruce for each side of the fireplace on the north.

After the corrals were built and new gate posts put in, Dick decided he needed a name for this new ranch. He picked the brand for his horses to be the ORO. I think he was thinking this was going to be his gold mine.

I was still learning how to cope with this new lifestyle. You don't forget your city upbringing in a few months. Not only were there the daily chores to do, but also the care of the garden and the canning. Canning was a hot job. I had hung a thermometer in the back of the tent and one afternoon when I was canning vegetables it got so hot the thermometer broke. There was no time to worry about hot weather. When the vegetables were ready to can, that's when you got busy and did it. We worked hard every day and every hour was put to good use. We went to town occasionally, but we had bought a six-month supply of groceries, so there was very little to get.

When the Slate Creek Ranger Station went in, some friends of ours, Clark Neeley and Roy Scriven, were hired as the first cooks. We visited them at the cookhouse several times that summer and when the season was over, Dick had learned how to make home brew. Friends of Clark and Roy would share their recipe with Dick. We had a cellar so we would have a place to put it. It wasn't long until Dick was busy in his spare time figuring out how it was done and the necessary equipment. Nothing was done right away, but it was in the back of Dick's mind that he would have to try it. He started gathering bottles from everywhere, along the road, you name it.

When he finally got around to making the brew, we

Roy Scriven and Clark Neeley. Clark was cook at the Slate Creek Ranger Station and Roy was cook's helper. They taught Dick how to make home brew. The photo was taken at the log cabin they were building at Cuprum, Idaho.

were never without it. Some of it was okay and some of it was so wild most of it went up in foam. It was kinda' fun, but sometimes, in later years, I often wondered if people came to see us or to drink our free beer. Once in a while I would make root beer for the kids.

Then, in August, a cloudburst hit the draw above our place, changing drastically the flat where the house, corrals, and barn were built. A mound of rock and mud had come down, covering the existing road. The county cleared the main road but we could no longer see the upper end of the flat. We had to drive over the debris to get to our garden. We had to make new Jeep tracks from the main road down one side of the mound onto the flat. We knew, after this experience, not to build anything where a draw came down.

Summer was almost over. The end of the garden was in sight. Everything in the garden was harvested except about 60 cauliflower plants. I spent one morning tying up the big leaves of the plants over the heads to bleach them white. When I left the garden, I fastened the gate and went to the tent feeling good. I would have lots of nice white heads of cauliflower to can and to sell. Next morning I went back up to the garden and what a sight. The neighbor's cows had torn down the fence and eaten every single plant. There went the spending money I planned on getting from the store.

But things were working out well for us. It wasn't long before Dick was going to work for Homer Rhett, packing hunters up John Day Creek. We would be able to get our winter's meat. We had worked hard all summer long and now the fall was upon us. When hunting season was over, we would be staying on the creek. Dick was not going to travel anywhere. When Christmas came, we went to New Meadows. After a few days of bitter cold in New Meadows, going back to the creek was a wonderful feeling.

SHOEING — 1951

The holidays were over and winter was upon us once again. It would be easier this time. We were settled in. Though water was still a problem when the creek froze, we would manage better. The house was a reminder that there was still plenty of work to be done.

One of Dick's friends wanted a relief from driving the Cow Creek school bus so Dick took that on for a while. It really wasn't very long until he realized he wasn't cut out to be a bus driver. He took the bus back and handed in the keys.

Meanwhile, he learned the Forest Service was offering a contract for a blacksmith to shoe all the horses and mules in the Nez Perce, Clearwater, and St. Joe Forests. Dick put in a bid and got it. Our summer work was lined up. All we had to do was wait until the job started.

When the weather warmed up Dick started breaking horses. He built another stockade corral, the third one. Then he built a loading chute from the road into the pasture. We cut more trees and built a log woodshed. Things were shaping up with a lot of hard work from both of us. We didn't put in a garden as we knew we would be gone most of the summer.

Dick was busy preparing for this shoeing job and soon he was on his first trip. While he was in Riggins and places south of Slate Creek, I was busy preparing the camp and getting the two-wheeled trailer packed. All meals had to be planned in advance as there would be few places to buy supplies. I can remember when this would have been a difficult task, but no more. I had turned pro.

To give an added importance to our camp trailer, I would put the nine-of-diamonds on it to hold the mantee down. It took a lot of rope and extra work, but it made a good conversation piece. I liked to show off whenever I got the chance. I still had a touch of smartness that I should have gotten over long before.

When Dick finished the first few days of shoeing, we hooked the trailer to our little red jeep and headed out. What an adventure. And what a way to see the whole of central Idaho, from the back roads.

We stayed on these back roads as much as possible. There would be back-tracking, as some roads didn't go clear through. What follows is the route we traveled on our trips.

When Dick finished in the Riggins area, we headed for Grangeville. We went down the Mt. Idaho grade to the South Fork of the Clearwater River and up that fork stopping at Castle Creek and Red River Ranger Station. We also stopped to shoe the Gertrude Maxwell stock and any others in between. Then on to Elk City and Dixie. From Dixie we back-tracked to Harpster and the Locksa River. Then we drove up the Locksa to the Selway River and up the Selway to Fenn Ranger Station and Selway Falls Guard Station. We always made it a point to arrive at the falls on a Friday so we could spend the week-end there. It was a lovely place to camp. Traveling through the back country was simply great.

From Selway Falls we retraced our route to Lowell and then north to Weippe, Pierce, and Headquarters. From Headquarters we followed the North Fork of the Clearwater to the Weittas and Kelly Forks. From Kelly Forks we traveled to Elk River, Clarkia, and Avery on the St. Joe

River. From Avery we climbed a mountain to Round Top and back down to Avery on the St. Joe and from there down the river to St. Maries, the end of the trip.

On our way home we took Highway 95 back to Moscow, Lewiston, and Grangeville. But before going on to Slate Creek we flew to Moose Creek Ranger Station with Frank Hill to shoe the stock there. This was a change from so much driving.

We had hit every ranger station, guard station, camp, trail, or wide spot in the road where there was Forest Service stock. If there was more to shoe than could be done in a day, we made camp. I was the one to unpack, set up the tent and stove, cut wood, and pack water. It was also up to me to cook the meals and help if there was no one else around.

Shoeing was hard work and I made sure I did everything I was expected to do and then some. If we were to move on that afternoon, we either had a cold lunch or I built a camp fire. Everything was well-organized. What a great summer. I was so glad for this job and for the chance to explore Idaho this way.

We only had a week between trips and then started in all over again. After the first trip we realized how close to Montana we had traveled and thought it would be nice, on the next trip, to sidetrack over to Glacier Park and visit our friends. If we took a few days off, we could work just a little harder and travel a little longer each day to make up for it. We wrote to our friends and told them of our plans and the date to expect us.

This trip, however, would be delayed by a freakish accident. While we were in White Bird getting our mail, Dick went to help one of his friends while I stayed in town to visit. While walking along the board sidewalk, I turned my ankle and broke a bone in my foot.

When Dick came to pick me up I had a foot ten times

as big as it should be and black as a crow. Dick said it would be okay in the morning as we had to take off on the next round.

Well, we didn't go the next day. I had to stay in the hospital under ice packs to get the swelling down so they could x-ray my foot. They found the break and put a cast on up to my knee with a walking heel. We left the next day, only one day late.

It was more difficult, however, for me to set up camp, cut wood, and pack water. But that was my job and I did it. It wasn't easy, but Dick's job wasn't easy either.

Then, on one trip, we decided to stay over a weekend in Dixie and do some fishing. We both had telescopic rods we always carried with us. We stayed in the Ward cabin, borrowed horses from the Forest Service, and took off for a good day of fishing.

My foot was still in a cast so it wasn't as easy riding as it could have been. I was also the one who had to carry all the excess baggage on my horse. There was always some reason Dick couldn't be encumbered, usually because of the kind of horse he was riding.

Anyway, I had the canteen, creel, and lunch. When we got to a good place to start fishing, I noticed the creek was lined with huge boulders. It was very difficult even to get to the creek. I decided I would ride my horse from place to place. I left my rod out full length and that way I didn't have to take it down each time.

There were lots of trees and brush along the creek also. Riding from one spot to another, I looked up the mountainside as I moved along and noticed three bears away high on the mountain slope. I didn't think they would see me from that distance, so I started down the trail. All of a sudden my horse spooked. The bears had come down the slope and crossed the creek. When I tried to hold my mare, she reared up, dumping me in the trail, and leaving my fishing pole hung up in the trees.

Boy, what a surprise! Luckily Dick was ahead on the trail or no telling where the horse would have gone or how far. We finally caught as many fish as we needed and went back to Dixie.

After that I wasn't too keen on fishing in that particular creek. Also, I kept a better watch for bears. I wished they had stayed up on the mountain, instead of deciding to come down.

On our next cycle, we finished the shoeing at Avery and Round Top and then headed for Montana, going through St. Regis, Thompson Falls, Kalispell and West Glacier. Dick had been working all day, so I drove while he slept. It was late afternoon when we started and we had a long way to go. I was barreling along at a good clip, rounded a curve in the road, and was faced by solid water.

I slammed on the brakes and came to a screeching halt. Dick woke up in surprise. There was water as far as we could see but we noticed lights on what was apparently the other side of the river. It was a ferry crossing! If there was a sign, I had missed it. When we got on the ferry we learned we were crossing the Clark Fork River.

We saw very little game on that trip and traveled many a mile without meeting another vehicle. We carried plenty of gas, and it's a good thing. The roads were long and lonely.

It seemed like that summer just flew by. We had traveled many, many miles through the back country of the three forests, a trip very few have had the opportunity to enjoy.

Everett Chaney, our friend from Horseshoe Bend on the Salmon River, wrote the following poem about Dick. It is published in Chaney's book called *Verse and Worse*.

Dick Sterling was shoeing a government mule;
He had already shod quite a few.
He nailed the shoes on, with a smile on his face,
Singing, "I get a kick out of you."

When the last of the 225 head of horses and mules were shod, Dick had done all the shoeing he wanted to for a while. He knew he would have a few head to shoe during hunting season, but nothing like the summer. Another summer had passed and we were looking forward to the fall season.

Hunting Camp at Buffalo Hump

It was fall, 1951. When the shoeing was over we got ready for hunting camp with the outfitter, Injun Rice. Dick would be doing the packing. This hunting and fishing camp was at Buffalo Hump in the high country, at an elevation of 8,924 feet. It had once been a big gold mining area. Injun had the base camps all set up and ready to go. We used an old mining shack for a cookhouse. It was sure handy to have a good, wood cookstove, table and chairs. Almost like uptown.

A creek ran through the meadow, making packing water easier. Wood was plentiful. The horses and mules were turned loose with the bell mare and a wrangle horse kept in the corral.

Dick shod the horses and mules and when that was finished we set up the spike camps. We cut and stacked wood at each camp, ready for the first hunters. There were many chores to do before the opening date.

Injun divided his season by using the high country first. The rest of the time was spent on the main Salmon River at Sheep Creek. Fishing was good in the high lakes and some of the hunts included a fishing trip along with the hunt.

When on the Salmon River, hunters were boated upriver from road's end above French Creek. Everything had to be portaged over Dried Meat Rapids. This was a big job and I always tried to avoid going by boat for that reason. Several trips were made up and down the river. The hunting continued until the first week in December.

When the season was over, we loaded the pack string and went up the trail to Moore's Cabin, stayed overnight, and continued on to Slate Creek the next day. If the top was snowed under, we went down the Salmon to Wind River and then on into Riggins.

We had come to the end of another fall and we would be at Slate Creek for the winter. We had been gone almost all summer and fall and it was time to get something done at home.

We were nice and cozy in our tenthouse. We still had the same problems as we had had the last winter with frozen water but some things had improved. Maybe this year we would be moving into our log house, but there was still a lot of work to do. With a new year coming up we had plenty to look forward to. We went to New Meadows again for the Christmas holiday.

GETTING READY FOR THE SNAKE RIVER

Most things Dick wanted to do around the place were already done. Besides the barn, we had now put up two log structures, the house and the woodshed. If I had paid attention, I would have realized there were changes coming on. But I was so set on staying on the creek and eventually getting the rest of the house built, that I was stunned when Dick started talking about the Snake

Pick and Lillie Ward on the Snake River Trail. Pick was the government trapper at the time Dick built the log bunkhouse at Kirkwood. Lillie was half Nez Perce Indian.

Pick and Lillie Ward at the Carter House. Bobcat hides, stretched and dried, are waiting to be packed out. The Carter House, known as Carter Mansion because it was more elaborate than any other place in the canyon, was where the government trapper stayed while working that area.

River, Pick Ward, and Pick's friend, Bud Wilson, who ran sheep at a place called Kirkwood. I didn't like this talk at all. Dick was far more acquainted with people than I. With his horse-breaking, people came from far and near. Pick and his wife, Lillie, had stopped many times to visit with Dick when he had horses around. Pick was the government trapper. He trapped for the Fish and Wildlife Service on the Snake River in the winter months and on the Salmon River and areas in the Payette National Forest in summer.

It must have been in their conversations that Dick learned Bud was needing a bunkhouse for his herders and his lambing and shearing crews. Dick became real interested and somehow got the idea that he'd like to meet Bud Wilson and talk to him about building the bunkhouse of logs. Dick would do the work.

When the bid came out for the 1952 summer shoeing job, he took the contract for the Nez Perce and Clearwater Forests only. The St. Joe Forest went to someone else. Our shoeing schedule would be the same as last year, except we would have three weeks at home between shoeing trips instead of just one week.

It wasn't long before Dick and Bud got together and the deal was done. Dick would build the bunkhouse in the fall after the shoeing was done. Many an evening was spent drawing plans for this building. He would get the logs in Lost Valley, cutting them during the three-week shoeing break.

In May a trip was planned up the Snake River. Helen and Bud Wilson, Pick and Lillie, and Dick and I would be going, starting the trip at Kirkwood and riding upriver on the Idaho side as far as Granite Creek.

It was on this trip that Dick bought an Appaloosa gelding from Pick to be my very own horse. We had acquired a couple of saddle horses that were only for Dick. Now I was the lucky one. Except, even though Chief was gentle, I kept thinking of the long trek to Granite Creek on a horse I'd never seen before.

We took a string of Bud's mules and the trip was wonderful. We stayed at Sheep Creek with Lenore Barton and her son Ace and then trailed on to Granite Creek to stay with Allen and Hazel Wilson and their son, Kim. Hazel had the most wonderful garden. Strawberries as big as teacups. I'd never seen anything in my life like it.

We were told fishing was great in Granite Creek and Sheep Creek and that trip up the river changed my mind somewhat about this move we were about to make.

Now we had plenty of work to do before the shoeing started. Dick finally got some lumber from the mill at Slate Creek and laid stringers and flooring in our log house. He took down the two tents and we moved the linoleum rugs and furniture into the house. Dick's folks gave us their old wood cookstove. A neighbor of theirs in New Meadows gave us a kitchen cupboard they had taken out of their home when they remodeled. It was at least eight feet long with shelves and drawers, and was counter high. It fit perfectly in one end of the cabin. We fixed the furniture so that we had four rooms in one. Dick built a door out of 1 x 12s and finished it with the boards on the outside to form a "z." We also had the traditional latch string. No one locked anything at that time. The Rural Electrical Association (REA) put in a single phase line. We then had Don Caward of Riggins come and put in the rest of the wiring.

Dick also built a lean-to porch on the house with lumber left over from the torn-down tenthouses. The windows we'd ordered came and they were put in. We didn't have the ceiling in, but that was minor and could be done later. Between shoeing trips we could finish what was most important before the big move.

In July, during the shoeing break, we went to Lost Valley to cut the logs for the bunkhouse. It would take 120 trees. This was a big job. We still had only a cross-cut saw and an axe to work with. Bud's brother, Lem, said he had a chainsaw we could borrow. That would be great, for me especially. He said he'd leave it at the Shell Station in White Bird and we could pick it up there. We were anxious to get started so we drove to White Bird. Sure enough, the saw was there, a Titan.

We got the gas and oil and headed home. This was a Saturday. That night the Shell station burned to the ground and, when Lem heard about it, he thought his chainsaw had burned too.

The next day we left for Lost Valley and unloaded our gear. Dick tried and tried to start the chainsaw but it refused to run. So we had to load up and go home. The next day we took the saw to White Bird and that's when we discovered the Shell station had burned. When Lem came through town and we returned his saw he wasn't very happy. He was sure he was going to get a new one from the insurance.

So much for being an eager beaver and not waiting to go to work. Now we had to settle for the cross-cut saw and I can tell you it was mighty hard on me. I only weighed about 95 pounds and Dick kept yelling at me to quit riding the saw. I didn't know what he meant and he'd get too mad to stop long enough to explain. He never did, but through hard work and plenty of cussin', we finally cut all 120 trees and bucked them up into 20-foot lengths.

We didn't peel the logs, but decked them and piled the brush, working every day until the job was finished. What time we had left was spent planning what we'd take to the Snake River. I wanted to take my Singer treadle sewing machine. By then I was making all our western shirts and there was always plenty of mending to do.

After the trees were cut, we continued the shoeing until the contract was completed in September.

THE SNAKE RIVER

Bud, Dick and Jack Neilson hauled the logs from Lost Valley to Kirkwood using Bud's three stock trucks. The logs had been cut so they wouldn't hang over too much for highway travel. The trip was approximately one hundred miles each way, which allowed only one trip a day. I rode with Bud most of the time. He was the lead truck and someone had to open the gates. It took several days to haul them all. We returned to Slate Creek to put business in order, secure the house, and ready things for the move. This would include a trip to the dentist in Council to have the rest of my teeth pulled. If possible, I would have to come out later to have the teeth fitted.

We filled the woodshed with wood. Our horses would be turned into the Tipton pasture across the creek. There was no fence along the creek so they could come back and forth as they wished. Every day the list of what to take to the river grew. This move would last longer, seven months, as it turned out.

The day to leave finally arrived. I'd seen the Jordan house we'd be living in and was excited about this new adventure. Dick was also happy; he was going to build a great log bunkhouse. We'd be getting $200 a month with room and board for this work, which included my time helping him and doing laundry and cooking for whoever was at Bud's place.

We met Bud at the town of Lucile and followed him into

Bud Wilson. This photo, donated by Clark H. Neeley, was taken during the time Bud owned Kirkwood Ranch.

the ranch.

Upon arrival, the first thing I had Bud do was remove the small, three-burner propane stove from the top of the big wood stove. I would use only wood.

Dick and Bonnie with Bud Wilson. This Polaroid picture of the Kirkwood house kitchen shows the phone, the corner cabinet and the large dining table. I kept the picture in my cookbook for many years so it is in poor condition. It was taken by Bud's brother, Vern Wilson.

Then Bud startled me by saying he had some friends coming in that day to hunt. Surprise! I hadn't even unloaded anything yet. Instead of having three for supper, I had seven. Somehow I got through it and the next day everything was put in order. I had no leisure time to get used to my new home.

When his hunters left, Bud asked Dick and me to go with him to his home in Nyssa, Idaho, to buy the winter's groceries. This made up for his having guests on the day we moved in. It was a great trip. We went to Ontario, across the state line in Oregon, to a wholesale grocery. Later, I asked Bud how much groceries cost to feed everyone all winter. He said over $2,000.

We returned to Kirkwood the next day and it took Bud and Dick no little time to unload the truck. Cases upon cases were stacked in the upstairs middle room. Things that wouldn't freeze or draw moisture were stacked on the screened porch. The next day Bud left for a week or so and we started to settle in.

That afternoon the camp tender, Harve Rush, rode in from up river. He moved onto the screened porch so we were a full house. Bud had his special bedroom, we had ours, and Harve on the porch.

The Jordan house was located close to Kirkwood Creek on the bench above the river. On the cement floor in the kitchen of the house sat a large Monarch woodstove with the water heater beside it. The water was heated by coils in the firebox of the stove. From the stove to the wall was a Mother Hubbard cupboard. Another cupboard just like it framed the stairwell going upstairs. From a window over the sink it was easy to spot anyone coming as they crossed the creek.

The dining area was furnished with a big table and ten chairs. My sewing machine and a corner china cabinet were also in the dining area.

Dick was good about keeping plenty of wood cut but no one helped me wash, iron, cook, or clean. Routine was one thing I knew I needed. After we were there a week, Bud came with a brand new Maytag gas engine washing machine. It was wonderful. Every Monday morning the "putt putt" of that motor was music to my ears. It was a beautiful machine and I took very good care of it.

Invited friends of Bud's popped in and out unannounced. When I started a meal, I never knew how many I would end up feeding. I would be glad when hunting season was over.

As soon as I finished my work each day I would go out

and help Dick put up the logs. Like before, when we were building, the canyon echoed with cuss words. I wasn't doing anything right. Since I was the only help he had, he had to put up with me. The logs were easier to handle because the bark had been left on. Many an hour I sat on logs with a draw knife taking the bark off. When the walls were five or six logs high, I refused to clamber up. I wasn't that good at balancing. Dick was like a cat, no problems with heights.

When he came to the log that would be the bottom or top of a window or door, he would cut out a space about four inches deep and level it off for placing the window or door. The entire opening would not be cut until the building had settled at least four months. The windows

Wenaha Mail Boat. The men are loading wool sacks at the upper boat landing at Kirkwood. Bud Wilson's small motorboat, the ocean-going Sea Scow, is tied nearby.

were big and would have to be made to measure.

Bud was in and out and the bunkhouse progressed every day. When it stormed, Dick had other chores to do. Harve came and went. We were lucky he was so congenial, a really swell fellow. Before the winter was over I found that, between Dick and Harve, there was always something cookin'. What one didn't think of, the other did.

We had been on the river almost two months when Bud came in and told us this would be his last trip in by road. Next trip he would boat up from Pittsburg. The weather was turning colder and it surely would snow before too many days.

After Bud left, Harve and Dick were sitting at the kitchen table drinking coffee when all of a sudden the conversation turned to going out to town one more time before the road snowed up. We hadn't been out since we

Hauling hay by boat. Bud and helpers load hay into the motorboat to take across the river at Big Bar. (Photo donated by Clark H. Neeley)

119

Bud boating hay across the Snake River in the Sea Scow. (Photo donated by Clark H. Neeley)

came in except the trip to Nyssa, and I hadn't planned on any more. But soon both Harve and Dick were rustling around getting their chores done and cleaning up. I was not going to be left behind.

When we figured Bud was well past Riggins on his way home, we started out. How exciting to be going out for dinner and seeing friends again.

We had a great time in Riggins. As we waited for Harve to finish his visiting, Dick leaned up against a one dollar slot machine at Summerville's. He took his last silver dollar and put it in the machine, saying, as he did, "I might just as well go back to the ranch broke." Instead, he hit the jackpot, $105. Suddenly, everybody was his friend, but he put one dollar back in the machine, gave me $52, rounded up Harve, and we left.

It had gotten much colder and on the way back we got started talking about the water, hoping it hadn't frozen in the house. Well, it had, but we went to bed figuring we'd do something about it when we got up.

At breakfast Harve had the bright idea to put the kerosene stove in the bathroom and light it to thaw out the cold water pipe going into the water heater. That we did, closed the door, and went about our chores.

About two hours later I went to see how the stove was doing. I opened the bathroom door and let out a scream at what I saw. Dick and Harve came running. The stove had gone out and black soot was everywhere. The white door, the white tub, the walls of the bathroom which had been covered with white oil cloth — all were black. You never saw such a horrible sight. The woodwork, towels, the whole room was filthy.

Immediately Harve said he was sorry he couldn't help clean up; he had to go to Granite Creek and off he went to get his mules. Dick finally got the water running and said he guessed he'd go with Harve. So the two of them took off, leaving me to clean up the mess. I was furious but couldn't do a thing to stop them. They stayed away for a week, giving me time to put everything in order again.

After I'd cleaned the bathroom, which took more than one day of scrubbing, I enjoyed the time by myself. I loved the solitude of the canyon and, other than the mail boat that came on Thursdays, didn't see a soul. Nor did I call Hazel Johnson at Temperance Creek or Joan Clay at Pittsburg. I was glad Dick and Harve were up the river, but was glad to see them return when the wood pile got low.

Since it was still hunting season, Dick and Harve had gotten a deer and I was more than pleased to see them. There was always plenty of mutton but deer were scarce along the river. That much would last us all winter. It was November and Dick was still working on the logs of the bunkhouse. This took part of my day too.

I got a letter from "Ma" Gerber, the dentist. Everyone that I knew called Dr. Gerber, "Ma." She told me that, since I couldn't come out to see her, she'd mail my teeth in to me. I'd been gumming it for over three months and I was anxious to have teeth again.

Thursday, Thanksgiving Day, the boat finally arrived. I let the men starve as I waited for the boat. My teeth *would* be on it. Well, I might just as well have had dinner on time. My new teeth had to come out for me to eat. I felt like I had a brick building in my mouth. It took several days to get used to all that molded matter.

Christmas came and went, with life having a definite pattern. Seemed like there was never a dull moment. If I had any free time I made shirts for both Dick and me.

Pick and Lillie Ward lived in the Carter house a mile up Kirkwood Creek. Lillie was half Nez Perce and half French Canadian. She had taught me how to make sourdough her way. Now I had plenty of time to experiment with it. I got to be very good at it before I left the river and was never without sourdough after that.

Lillie came into the house one day when I was ironing with the sadirons which had to be heated on the stove. She said she had a Coleman gas iron I could use. She'd go get it. She got on her horse and soon rode back with the iron. It was wonderful not to continually change irons as they heated and the job was much easier.

That winter it got below zero a time or two and snowed a few times. The creek froze over but the water from the creek into the house continued to flow.

We had no radio so we only knew of the outside world from mail we received. Oliver McNabb was the mail boat pilot on the "Wenaha." This boat, slower than the ones they have now, made seven knots an hour coming up from Lewiston. There was no set place to camp overnight. Oliver pulled in anywhere it was convenient when it got dark.

Oliver used to let me ride up to Sheep Creek and back whenever no one was around to cook for. He never charged me but I didn't get to do it too often.

If Hazel Johnson was at Temperance Creek I would telephone her and tell her I would be on the boat. She would come to the landing if she had time and we would visit while freight was being loaded or unloaded. Then I would continue on up the river to Sheep Creek and back. It was a fine way to see the country. There were no other people living on the river by this time; the other places had all been bought out by Bud.

I didn't ride a horse that winter. My job was in the kitchen. I didn't even fish, but I sure made up for it in later years. I did walk along the river sometimes and every time I'd cross the sand bar, I'd find arrowheads, some good, some not so good. But I'd keep them just the same.

Bud would boat up from Pittsburg a couple of times a month and on one trip he asked me if I'd cook for lambing and shearing. He'd pay me extra. This extra would be mine, all mine. No sharing. So I agreed. Bud had the road opened in February and supplies came in to get ready for the big operation.

Dick was lucky and didn't have to help with the sheep shearing. He was still putting the finishing touches on the bunkhouse. Bud brought in Jim Davis of Lucile to help raise the rafters, put on the sheathing and roofing, and help with the ceiling.

When all the bands of sheep were gathered and everyone got to Kirkwood, I ended up with 27 men to cook for. It was a little crowded but we did fine. Dick always helped by keeping the wood box filled and giving me a helping hand cutting meat.

I told Bud we would have to have a schedule for the meals and he said that was impossible. No sheep outfit ever had a schedule and I told him this one was going to be the first.

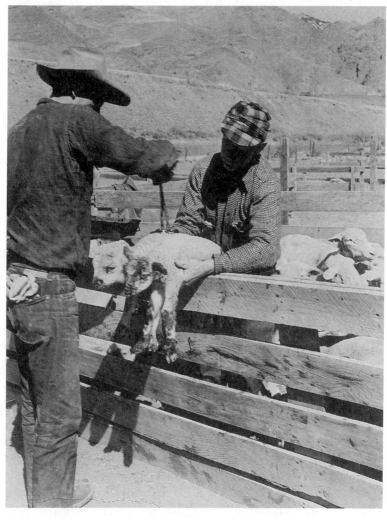

Branding lambs. Morris Kohlhepp and Henry Bowen are branding lambs at Big Bar. (Photo donated by Clark H. Neeley)

When the shearers arrived, my schedule for the next six weeks was set. At 4 a.m., while Dick built a fire, I dressed, made the bed, and was ready for work. Two 25-cup pots of coffee steamed on the woodstove. Dick sliced bacon and I mixed up sour dough for hotcakes. I cooked cereal and got out the eggs. By 5:30 a.m. the first ten sat down at the table. Then, as each one finished eating, I'd take his plate, silver and cup to the sink full of hot water, wash, rinse and dry them, and put them back on the table. We only had ten plates.

I fried hotcakes and eggs as the working men came in. When they were fed, visitors or wives of herders ate. I very seldom stopped to eat. I ate on the run.

Bud bought all the flour in 25-pound sacks. As soon as

Left-handed sheep shearers. All four of these shearers from Bill Dorman's crew were left handed. The are (L. to R.) Russel "Bud" Cooper, Larry Garver, Don Leeper, and Bill Dorman. (The photo, donated by Clark H. Neeley, was taken at Kirkwood)

Del Catron, sheep herder, at camp.

breakfast was over, I mixed up the sourdough biscuits for the noon meal. It took 25 pounds of flour every other day. They ate at noon sharp. Then the kitchen was cleaned up and the evening meal started. Referred to as "supper," it was served at 6 p.m. The night men on the lambing crew ate at 11 p.m.

I had a long day and a short night. I tried to save the time between 3 and 4 p.m. every day for myself to catch up on what I wanted to do. Or I made pie shells for the next day's cream pies. Every pie, cake or cookie was made from scratch. Even if I do say so now, the men were well-fed and I was turning out to be one heck of a good cook. I was getting plenty of practice.

When the bummer lambs came along, Bud brought them up to a pen near the house and I had them to feed too. My days were planned for the same thing: Monday, wash, Tuesday, iron, Wednesday, mend, and always there was baking. I really worked hard.

When Bill Dorman and his shearing crew left and most of the sheep had been lambed out, Dick and I decided, since we weren't going to continue on for the summer, that it was time to load up our two-wheel trailer and head for Slate Creek. We were going to summer in Glacier Park. Dick had a packing job with the Park Service.

Lambing and shearing sheds. Shown with the canvas on, these sheds were used during lambing and shearing times. When the season was over, everything except the framing was taken down. The canvas was rolled up and hauled out for storage.

It had been a wonderful fall, winter and spring. Dick had completed his log bunkhouse, cut out the openings, and was ready to leave.

When we left the river, I returned the Coleman iron to Lillie. The next trip to town I bought one for myself. I knew sooner or later I would be needing one again.

When we got back to Slate Creek it felt good to be home again, even though I knew it wasn't going to last very long. In a couple of months we'd be heading for Montana.

During the summer, while we were in Montana, Bud and a helper hauled rock from up the creek for the bunkhouse floor. This raised the floor level so that cement could be poured. Then a cement porch was added with iron pipe imbedded for hitch racks. Dick had given Bud the measurements to have the doors and windows made. By the time October came around and the sheep were trailed in for the winter, life there started again. The bunkhouse was ready for use.

GLACIER NATIONAL PARK

Dick was a great letter writer. He wrote all the letters to our friends. All winter he had corresponded with Bill and Doris Yenne who had moved back to Glacier National Park, Montana, from Grand Canyon.

As it turned out, Bill got Dick a summer job packing and shoeing for the Park Service. He'd be working regular hours five days a week and weekends free. We would enjoy more social life than with other jobs we'd had. It was going to be a great summer.

We took our own camp, duffle bags, bed rolls, shoeing tools, saddles, and all our personal needs for the summer. We also took lots of canned foods from the cellar. We were excited about seeing new country and were most impressed with the beauty of the park when we arrived in West Glacier.

The first few days were busy. We moved into a government cabin. I thought the summer was going to be just great living in a house with running water.

But we soon found out we were going to live at Two Medicine. The first thing we had to do was take a truckload of horses and mules to the pasture there. Two Medicine is at the opposite side of the park from headquarters and we were the first ones to cross over on the Going-To-The-Sun Highway that summer. The road had just been opened and there was still a lot of snow along the sides. The ragged peaks glistening white in the snow sure were pretty.

We returned to West Glacier and packed up our belongings again to move. I remember on the way over we saw a bunch of Mountain sheep. Dick stopped the jeep and we decided we would see how close we could get to them. They just stood and watched us climb up the trail. They weren't the least bit scared of us and they acted as if they were waiting for us to take their picture. They probably had seen more people get out of their cars to take pictures than we could imagine. We didn't go too far, as it was rough going. And it was cold for July.

We moved into another Government cabin at first, but before long Dick decided it would be more convenient for him if we set up a tent near the corrals.

So much for living where there was a faucet of running water. I had lived in a tent for two and a half years, so that wasn't new to me. I just thought that this summer would be different. In our tenthouse we had a floor, so this would be more like hunting camp, only a different place.

One thing about Dick, when he got a job somewhere, he always went prepared. So when we set up the tent, we had with us the Coleman lantern, gas can, axe, and camp stove. We never left home without them.

The following information about Dick's duties for the summer was obtained from correspondence with Charles "Jack" Potter, an assistant park ranger of Glacier National Park today. He informed me that the duties now are relatively the same as when we were there, except some of the places we had packed to are either torn down or abandoned. One such station, Waterton, flooded in 1964 and a new station was built.

Dick's job had many duties. He would be packing in supplies and equipment for trail-maintenance crews throughout the park. Also, he'd pack in lumber and planks for bridges, walkways, and outhouses as well as

Crossing Two Medicine River. Dick is taking a pack string across Two Medicine River in Glacier National Park.

supplies and repair materials for lookouts.

He was to keep the stock shod. The summer would be busy doing the kind of work Dick especially liked since it was mainly packing. Sometimes he had to help build fence and other chores when needed.

I went with Dick whenever possible. If he was working with a crew some place, I stayed in the tent. There was always plenty to do to keep up with washing, ironing and cooking.

I remember when we went to the Waterton Ranger Station to shoe the stock there. We had to travel first to Waterton, Canada, and then back to Montana by boat down Waterton Lake to the Ranger Station.

Joe, the ranger, was to meet us at a given time and place. We arrived in Waterton early, so decided to explore the town. As we walked along I noticed a sign that said

"The Dime Store." I told Dick I wanted to go in, as I hadn't been in a dime store in a long time. There were no other signs saying it was anything different.

We walked in the front door and, to our surprise and everyone else's in the room, we were in an old fashioned bar with absolutely no tables and chairs or stools at the bar.

We were so embarrassed we weren't sure just what to do. So, as the patrons at the bar stared, we walked calmly through the long bar, looking neither right nor left, and on into a room we could see in the back that had tables and chairs.

When the waiter came over to take our order Dick said we'd have a "glass of beer." The guy looked at us like we were stupid and walked off to get our beer. As we sat and watched, others came in the back door. We noticed that everyone was brought two glasses of beer which was thumped down loudly by the waiter. I guess we were supposed to order two beers. When we left by the back door we decided it wasn't a good idea to try any more stores unless we knew for sure what they were.

Before long Joe came along at the appointed place and we left for the ranger station.

We spent a wonderful time there. Everyone went fishing, and for once I caught the biggest fish, a Mackinaw trout. This spoiled Joe's record; he'd always caught the biggest fish. I'd used a goofy lure that Dick told me wouldn't catch anything. It was orange with black spots. When we got back to Two Medicine we had a big fish feed at our tent.

I remember one day in particular. I was riding the trail, went around a bend and came face to face with a moose. I don't know who was more frightened, me or the moose. I was lucky the animal turned and ran. I was a little more watchful after that, as moose were plentiful and could be dangerous.

When the huckleberries were ripe we followed a trail regularly where the bushes were taller than my head when I sat on my horse. As we rode through we would stop and fill my lunch sack in just a few minutes. We learned after the first time or two to take sacks for the berries. They were the biggest I had ever seen.

After the day's work was done, Dick liked to go to the dump and watch the grizzly bears. They were numerous and spent most of their time at the dump feeding on garbage. You had to be very careful but it was fun to watch them.

We met a lot of nice people that summer and it seemed like the time just flew by. When you're only going to spend four months in one place it goes fast. I believe Glacier National Park is one of the most beautiful places I have ever been. But when it came time for hunting season back home, Dick quit his job. We packed up our camp and supplies and left. Once more we were going home.

Buffalo Hump — 1953

After arriving at Slate Creek, we started preparing for the next two and a half months in the Buffalo Hump hunting camp. We loaded our two-wheel trailer with all the supplies we needed and other things Injun Rice had left word for us to bring in.

It took a good long day to go in. We went to Grangeville and down the Mount Idaho grade to the South Fork of the Clearwater River. From there, we headed up the South Fork to just beyond Golden, then turned off to Orogrande. Then we followed the primitive road to the Orogrande Summit and on to the Hump. From the summit on it wasn't even what some people would call a primitive road.

There were several mines in the area. Some of the names were Orogrande, Calendar, Vesuvius, Concord, Cracker Jack, and others. At one time it was a booming gold mining area.

One nice thing about hunting camp is that you meet new people every year, along with the ones who come back year after year. Some of the hunters brought in their own groceries and cooked for themselves. Others wanted to hire a cook, a job which always fell to me. I didn't mind, as I liked being away from the main camp. That way I got to see more of the country.

It seemed as though more unusual things happened in a spike camp than in the base camp. One such incident occurred when we had some hunters at a spike camp up

Sheep Creek. The weather was unusually warm during the day, but cooled off at night. I had a cold-box in the creek to keep things cool. I had warned the hunters that if they took anything out of the cooler, to be sure it s lid was to be kept on when the container was not being used.

Things went well for a few days. Then, on a particularly hot day, the hunters came in tired and thirsty. The blow flies had been real bad every day, but by warning the hunters to keep lids on containers, we did fine. This particular day the fellows decided to get the can of tomato juice out of the creek cooler and have a nice cool drink. They must have had something to add to it, as they kept the can in their tent quite a spell. At what time they returned the juice can to the cooler, I don't know.

I only know that the following morning I took the tomato juice out of the cooler, set it on the table, and waited for the hunters to come in for breakfast. When they did, the first one poured himself out a glass of juice, passed it to the next fellow, and on to the third fellow. This time, out of the can came a big gob of blow flies. That was the end of breakfast and the last time any of the fellows forgot to put a lid on anything they took out of the cooler. What a way to start a day!

When the season was over at the Hump, we had Injun's son drive our jeep and our two-wheel trailer to White Bird. He was then supposed to drive it to the end of the road above French Creek to be used for hauling the last of the camp to White Bird. When we got to Sheep Creek we learned that the trailer had been lost somewhere between the Hump and Grangeville. We were always puzzled how anyone could miss not hearing the rattle of an empty trailer being pulled behind a little army jeep. Oh, well.

We always got our winter's meat and taking care of it would be the next big job when we returned to Slate Creek. All too soon another hunting season was over.

TUCSON

At Slate Creek, the horses and mules were taken care of. The meat we had gotten in hunting camp was hung, cured, then canned or cut and wrapped for the freezer. We had new plans for the winter and were anxious to get started. We would be wintering in Tucson, Arizona. Dick's letter writing had given us a new place to go. Some hunters from the Hump had invited us to come and spend some time with them on our way to Arizona. We closed our house once more.

I don't remember where in California we went, but I know we spent several days. The people we stayed with had a beautiful big old rambling hacienda, with magnificent furnishings, I remember. We did have a very good time before continuing on to Arizona.

Ray Milligan had been a guide for Fred Harvey at Grand Canyon. Now he was working for Zary South's Western Store as a saddlemaker. His wife, Liz, worked in a factory. I remember very little of the trip to Tucson. We had traveled so much it is now difficult to recall all the trips clearly.   When we got there I got a job as clerk at Zary South's and Dick worked breaking horses.

Some Sundays we would all go to Nogales, Mexico, to have lunch. This was truly exciting. I had never seen so many photographers as I did there, all wanting to take our picture. If you kept turning them down, sooner or later they'd get in a big argument among themselves.

One Sunday, Ray was looking for a particular restaurant. Most Mexicans we stopped to ask couldn't understand Spanish and none of us could speak Mexican. We finally learned that most people close to the border speak a mixture of English, Spanish, and Mexican.

Before the day was over we found the restaurant named "Hole in the Wall." No other name would have fit. It was a natural cave with dark and gloomy lighting, an unusual setting.

We mainly just wandered from store to store and watched other people. It was a good relaxing way to spend a Sunday. On Sundays, in Tucson, there was always a jackpot rodeo going on close by. Most of the rodeo cowboys winter here in Tucson. The weather was perfect.

After six weeks, Dick's job was over and he hired out to cowboy on a ranch up in the mountains above Patagonia. I quit my job but I was hired to cook at the ranch. I found myself at a huge rambling hacienda, with thick, three-foot walls, dim lighting, and the biggest wood cookstove I had ever seen. I had to cook for eight Mexicans who couldn't speak English. Even my high school Spanish didn't do much good.

It was really trying to come up with some kind of communication. I never asked Dick to explain how he got along, but with lots of gestures, like hand movements and always laughter, I thought it was a great experience. The food I had to cook there was red beans and potatoes, a few vegetables, and dried apples, pears and peaches. Coffee, too, of course, and I added some baked goodies, which pleased the men. We got along fine.

When the weather began to get hot in February we headed north again. This time we came back up to the Grand Canyon to visit our friends before leaving Arizona, then on through Bryce and Zion National Parks, places we'd never seen before.

Fixing Up the Place & a Survey Job
(Spring of 1954)

It was early spring and great to be home again. We'd spent a fun winter in Arizona but now it was time to do some work around the place.

This summer Dick decided he would finally get the Forest Service to mark some trees for logs to build the addition on the existing house. This time we would get the logs up the Free Use Road above White Bird. I can't remember the exact spot but it was a shorter haul than going back to Lost Valley.

Dick hired Wayne Claar of White Bird to haul the logs. He had a lot of help that day from men around White Bird who had heard about the log hauling. For once I was relieved of the hard work. The logs were dumped along the fence just inside the pasture, easy access for the work ahead.

Before starting this log job we splurged and bought a chainsaw, a Homelite. Nothing was safe around the place after that. Dick was like a kid with a new toy. But what a relief it was for me to be able to hang up the crosscut saw.

Still, tempers were the same as on any job we did that required heavy physical work. Dick and I got along quite well when we were on the river. It was when we were out among other people that we had more problems. Since we

138

both had tempers it didn't take much to light a fuse. They say true love doesn't run smooth, and I guess whoever said that knew what she was talking about.

During this time, Dick's folks came down and brought us a used Maytag washing machine. It worked fine except that it didn't have a wringer. I was glad to get any kind of

Bonnie and Dick at Slate Creek.

machine as long as the washing part worked. Now all I had to do was pack water, fill the machine, and put in a small electric heater we had bought. It was about five inches in diameter and took about three hours to heat the water. It worked and that was the main thing. Dick built a platform out behind the house for the machine and a bench to put the laundry tubs on. Things were sure getting fancy around this place. Since we had a single-phase electric line to the house we still had to watch how many things we plugged in at the same time. The Rural Electric Association would put in another line when we had the required work done on the wiring.

Ike Stock of Riggins made us two corner bookcases that fit on either side of the fireplace. We were slowly getting the things done that Dick thought were the most important. These things weren't always the same as I wanted, though.

When Dick worked at something he really wanted to do, he worked like the devil himself was looking down his shirt collar. I think all the time he was working on one job, he was thinking about what he was going to do next. Or maybe where he wanted to go next.

The tongue and groove flooring he had put down in the house was coming apart at the seams. It was green when we got it from the mill and, as it dried, it didn't stay the way it was. It had been in for two years and it would be many more years before a permanent floor would be put in.

Several weeks had passed since our return from Arizona. The next thing to do was to tear down the GI school barn. Dick needed a tack shed more than he needed a barn. With all the work I did in the house, I was still expected to help with anything Dick was doing that needed an extra hand.

Dick built the shed adjoining one of the three stockade

corrals. He poured a cement floor and foundation before putting up the logs. This made a good, sturdy building. Afterward he took the leftover logs and put a fence up around the yard to keep the horses from hanging around the house. He also built a panel gate. We now had good fencing to keep our horses and those we were breaking from wandering.

We planted two clump birch, one on each side of the shed door. Dale Tipton gave us two fast-growing trees-of-heaven. In years to come we would have lots of shade around the house.

The place was beginning to look like a real ranch. With the big gate posts and the hanging sign that said "THE ORO RANCH" it looked most impressive. Oro is Spanish for gold and ORO was our horse brand.

Midway through the season, Dick heard about a job packing a survey crew up Partridge Creek. A new road was to be built up the creek to join an existing road coming from the other side of the mountain. Dick bid on it and, like always, he bid so low he was sure to get it. We hired another fellow to help with the packing and I was the camp cook. That was included in Dick's bid.

This was a job that would only last a few weeks or so. We hauled our camp to the Howard Ranch on the main Salmon. The stock was trailed in from Slate Creek.

Dick took care of the saddle horses which the surveyors rode and packed all the supplies needed for each day's work. All the survey equipment was packed back to the camp each evening and out again in the morning. We moved camp every day or so to keep up with the crew. This was a lot of work, but it was fun seeing new country.

All the men took a lunch which I prepared while they were eating breakfast. Dick wasn't too happy about carrying a lunch but he had no choice. Each time we moved camp and climbed higher in the mountains, it

141

took longer to get to the spot where they had ended their survey the night before. Finding a camping spot became more difficult with each move.

We set up sleeping tents and a cook tent at each new camp. With our experience and camping equipment, we had a well-organized camp. We knew what to have and what not to have. The survey crew was very pleased with our arrangements.

The higher we got, the more difficult it was to pack water. The stream became smaller and the banks steeper. This made camp chores more difficult.

Trees and brush had to be cleared for the right-of-way for their survey line and Dick helped with this. I always thought it would have been fun to go with them one day and watch the proceedings. Of course, that was impossible because of my camp duties. Everything took longer in a camp situation where wood and water had to be packed and clean-up was more difficult.

The weather was beautiful. We were lucky not to have any bad thunderstorms. It was a new experience in some ways, yet still camping.

About every other day, the packer Dick had hired had to return to Riggins for supplies. As the days passed and we moved farther away it took the packer longer to go to town for fresh vegetables, meats, and bread. These surveyors liked to eat just like they did at their homes. No rough cookouts for them.

One such time when the packer didn't return in the two days allotted for supplies, I knew I was going to have to use the meat that I had in camp. It was nice t-bone steaks. They just hadn't kept in this hot weather, even though I kept everything in the creek in a cooler box.

I waited until I knew I had to do something with the meat. I took a dish pan and went to the creek, filled it with the cold water, and carried it uphill to camp. I added a cup

of vinegar and put the steaks in. After an hour I had changed the water several times.

When it was time to fry the steaks, they didn't smell too bad. The fellows thought they were great and wondered why I wouldn't eat a nice, tender t-bone steak. I knew, but never told any one. No one got sick, either.

When we hit the top of the mountain and met the road from McCall, we weren't needed anymore. We packed up camp and headed back down the mountain to the Howard Ranch where we had left our jeep.

The packer brought the mules and horses to the rodeo grounds in Riggins and left them in the corrals over night. Next day I drove Dick back to get the stock and bring them to Slate Creek. Our job was finished.

Then Dick decided we would go into the Hump early. It was two months earlier than we had ever gone in before. This way we could see what it was like during the season when Injun had fishing parties.

Since we had lost our two-wheel trailer, we decided to buy a truck to haul in all the supplies at once. We went out to Grangeville and put down a payment on a REO truck, got a six-month license, and were in business. We made more than one trip into the Hump, but it did save a lot of time.

The hunting camps were put out early. We had many fishing parties and the rest of the summer passed very quickly.

Then fall and the hunting season was upon us. With new and old friends showing up, the season came into full swing. Like before, when the early part of the hunting was over, we moved to the camp on the main Salmon River at Sheep Creek.

When the hunting was over, we returned to Slate Creek to spend the rest of December at home. We had only spent one Christmas on the creek since we'd been there.

Two Summer Jobs

We hadn't planned anything for this winter, just decided to enjoy time at home.

We bought a freezer and put it in the shed, a fine addition. No need to go to Riggins to a locker for our meat. Nothing new was acquired for the house. Those things would come later. We had the basic necessities.

Winter passed and Dick broke a few horses while he decided what to do next. As it turned out, we were home all summer. Dick went to work for McNutt Construction Co. They were doing road work along the main Salmon River between John Day Creek and Lucile.

For McNutt, he drove one of those huge Euclid dump trucks. I was amazed at his courage. Every now and then he really did something that was so unlike him. In this case, he traded his cowboy boots for heavy work shoes. The cowboy hat became a hard had. I do think he could have done anything he set his mind to.

I was happy to stay at home. The washing machine, without the wringer, was a great help. I had put the Coleman iron away for camp use only and had purchased an electric one.

No big jobs were accomplished the rest of the summer. Working nights was not the best choice, but few were eager to do it. Dick was on the graveyard shift. He didn't do any work during the day and there was not much you could do in the evening. It was a hard schedule to get used to. I was glad the job wasn't a lengthy one.

When the road job ended we did get lots of work done, but some of the things I wanted most were never finished. Seemed like Dick would get all excited about doing something and then lose interest if he thought it wasn't that important. I didn't dwell on the fact that we had no running water or the modern bathroom, but I thought that those things could have been considered as jobs to do around the place.

Then Dick learned that a contract was out to clearcut some forest land. He bid on it and got the job. That was one hard job. I thought some of the other things we had done were hard work, but this was something else. I was toughened up and knew how to do hard work but this was more than that. It was almost physically impossible for me, but I knew better than to complain. This meant money coming in.

I had the job of carrying the gas can, axe, canteen, lunch, and extra tools needed. Dick took the chainsaw and went like lightning through the trees, one after another, waiting only long enough for the tree to fall. It was steep; I could hardly stand up, let alone try to keep up with him. It was another one of our jobs where the only words Dick knew were to cuss me out for not doing my part.

It was not only hard to lug all that stuff, but also a scary place. The trees creaked, swayed, moaned and groaned. The wind always blew and you had to watch out for other trees falling because of the vibration and noise of the saw.

Dick would have been better off dragging a mule around. I darn near killed myself helping him and I don't think he ever realized what a hard time I was having. He absolutely had no patience with anyone who couldn't work like he did. I finally realized I was never going to be able to do all the things he expected of me. We worked

145

every day of the week, as there was a set time the job was supposed to be completed. He never bid on another job like that and I think, if he had, I would have refused to be his helper. He would have been kinder to someone else.

All in all, I had to admire Dick for his constant search for work of some kind. He really never wanted a job where he had to report at a given time. He wanted to be free of permanent obligations, to come and go as he pleased. I could go along or stay, that was up to me.

THE CASE OF THE MISSING QUAIL

After the clearcutting job, I kept wondering about the logs that lay out in the field and just when the new addition was going to start. A hunting camp was not mentioned when fall came. We just did the daily chores and were more or less at loose ends. Things weren't going too good on the creek.

When sheep-shipping time started in New Meadows, Dick hired out to Bud to pack sheep camps to the Snake River through the Seven Devils. I stayed home. Dick took my horse with him.

I decided that what the place needed was a nice, green lawn. I'd never had a lawn and didn't realize what had to be done to get one and keep it up. I bought some bluegrass seed and then found out you have to dig up the ground first, level it off, and then plant the seed. There was quite a big area around the house, but Dick was gone and I had to have something to keep busy. I dug up the whole yard, all the way around the house, removed the rocks and raked it level. What a back-breaking job! I planted the grass seed and thought of the wonderful job I had done.

One day I went to White Bird for the mail. There was a letter for me from my mother-in-law asking me if I would like to come to Boise and help her pick ducks. She had more work than she wanted to take care of. Since I was alone, it would be a good time to go and I could make some extra money for myself. I would get fifty cents a bird. I had never picked ducks before but I figured I could learn the process.

Everything went fine until it came time to package the ducks and quail. I must have had fifty ducks and maybe twenty quail to do. Then I ran into trouble, but I didn't know it was going to happen.

When I started to wrap the ducks and quail in freezer paper, I thought how tiny the quail were. I never gave a thought to who had purchased the plastic sacks, freezer paper, or tape. I thought how much a waste it was to wrap a quail, so I put each quail in a plastic bag and inserted it into the cavity of a duck. I also never gave a thought as to how the hunters would divide the birds when they got to California. My thoughts ran to conserving materials. I had always had to watch that. So that's what I did with all the quail and never thought to mention it to my mother-in-law either.

When my part of the job was finished and I was paid off, I returned home. A week later I got an emergency call at Burrows Store at Slate Creek. I was to call my mother-in-law immediately. I couldn't figure out what the trouble could be, so I drove down to the pay phone at Slate Creek and made the call.

Boy, was I surprised at the angry person on the other end of the line. First thing she asked me was, "Where are the quail you dressed and packaged for the hunters?"

"In the cavity of the ducks," I told her.

Wow! Did I ever get it then. The hunters had returned to California and when they took their birds out of the box they couldn't find any quail. They thought she had stolen them and were mad as hornets, and she was mad at me. When I tried to explain why I wrapped them that way she hung up on me.

I never once gave it a thought about how they were

going to divide the birds. I was thinking about saving. So the worst part of the whole thing was that the hunters had to thaw every duck to get the quail out. I had not marked the packages that had a quail inserted in the duck cavity either. I never picked another duck or quail for a hunter after that.

I'm glad I was many miles from all involved. My mother-in-law had spent many years building up a fine reputation for cleaning and packaging and taking birds to a special place the hunters had rented for freezing their birds. In one fell swoop I ruined her business. She had to give up the job because, I guess, word traveled fast among bird hunters.

I think it was months before my mother-in-law would speak to me kindly. Can't blame her though. I learned a valuable lesson. Don't ever hire out to pick ducks.

After the duck episode, I got a job in White Bird at the new Shell Station. I was a gas station attendant, fry cook, waitress and bartender and had to keep a watchful eye out for those playing pool. All that for seventy-five cents an hour, the going wage.

During this time my grass seed was beginning to sprout. I packed many a bucket of water to make sure it did. I was determined to have a green lawn. I had worked too hard at that back-breaking job for it to fail now.

After I'd worked awhile at the station I moved into a small trailer that was set up nearby. Then I didn't have to drive the ten miles to Slate Creek after closing hours every night. Sure was handy.

I had brought plenty of clothes and all that was needed to stay in White Bird, so I didn't return to Slate Creek. I forgot all about the grass. In the meantime it grew and grew and grew. Weather and rain were perfect. When Dick came out from the river, he saw my hay field and was furious. The grass had dried and turned into a fire hazard. When he came to White Bird to see me he wasn't the least bit impressed with my lawn. We didn't have a lawn mower, so why plant grass seed?

He said I was needed on the Snake River and to quit my job and return with him. Since I was more or less in the doghouse, I decided it was probably the best thing for me to do.

Guess who had to take the scythe and cut all the tall grass down before we left? Without any help from him. The harder I worked the madder I got. I never planted another grass seed as long as I lived on Slate Creek. Once was enough. After that, what came up was fine. With no watering during the summer months, what grew was sparse. Oh well, you live and learn. Sometimes it doesn't pay to get up in the morning.

SNAKE RIVER AGAIN

It didn't take long to pack what I needed for the winter and spring. I took my saddle, knowing I would have a chance to ride this time. We drove Bud's jeep into the ranch.

It felt good to be back at the familiar place on the river. The three big shade trees next to the house had lost their leaves. The screened meathouse out back of the house had a winter's supply of bacon hanging in it. It looked like someone had been digging in the garden spot for angle worms sometime during the summer. The bunkhouse was a welcome sight.

Pick and Lillie Ward were again at the Carter house up Kirkwood Creek where the government trapper stayed. Most everyone who had been on the ranch before would be there this year, too. There would be some new herders, as there seemed to be a constant turn-over for these lonely jobs. This year the herders were Morris and Dorothy Kohlhepp with Henry Bowen at Granite Creek, and Del Catron at Lightning Creek. Also there was Bill and Irene Winters, the Basque, Domingo, and one named Raymond Blanco. Harve, Albert Crawford, Jim Russell, and Henry and Jay Jones were some others. This was quite a crew, all with their separate camps.

It didn't take long to settle in. We went with Bud again to Nyssa to buy the winter's groceries. Bud not only furnished groceries, he furnished Camel cigarettes by the carton, Prince Albert, Velvet, Bull Durham and gloves. For fresh vegetables we had potatoes, carrots, and cabbage. There were no onions. Bud didn't like them. He didn't know there was a sack of them and plenty of garlic under our bed that would last the winter. There was never a pot of beans cooked while I was there that didn't have both onions and garlic in them. No one but Dick and I knew, but everyone, including Bud, thought my beans were great. What you don't know can't hurt you. Bud never had a sick day from eating them.

Another thing he didn't like was chicken. He said it gave him a pain in his shoulder. He bought chicken noodle soup by the dozen cases, though. He just didn't want us to buy a chicken to fry or roast. He probably had plenty at home. We brought in chicken from our cellar that I had canned, but he never knew.

The kitchen had changed some. The corner china cupboard was gone and another, larger cupboard was added. But the biggest change was the huge kerosene refrigerator. It was a sight to behold. How lucky we would be this winter. The fuel tank had to be refilled every seven days so it wouldn't run out of kerosene. If it did, it took a bit of doing to light it again. I filled it every five days and it never went out.

Bud had brought in an over-stuffed chair and that was a new addition. Good thing I left my sewing machine at home; there would have been no room for it in the kitchen. The telephone was still on the wall between the two windows, so I could call down the river to Pittsburgh.

Our groceries included 25-pound sacks of flour in pretty cloth materials. I would go through the piles of sacks and pick out those that matched so that I could make curtains and cupboard drapes for this house, Sheep Creek, Squaw Creek, and later on for the Carter house. They also made good dish towels. Nothing ever went to waste.

For winter, the weather was pleasant and mild on the river most of the time. It could get down below zero, freeze everything up, and snow, but as soon as the storms were over, it didn't take long for it to be beautiful again. The days flew by. Dick had some misgivings this time about the coming February. He would have to help round up the sheep. Before, he was working on the bunkhouse and got out of it.

We tried all winter to get a catalog from either Sears Roebuck or Montgomery Ward. The only answer was, if we sent an order, we would get a catalog. How can you make out an order unless you have a catalog? No matter how many letters we sent explaining about our location, we didn't even get a sales flyer. The herders who needed shirts, underwear, socks or other items they had forgotten when they were in New Meadows, sent letters out to Enterprise, Oregon, to Jack Wagner and Dexter Yokum to purchase their supplies and put them in the mail so they arrived before the boat left Lewiston. Bud did a lot of shopping for his men also. Everyone had to help each other.

This winter I would have a chance to go on a few trips with Dick when he went to the sheep camps. I really hadn't been anywhere except the area around Kirkwood and that trip up the river before we built the bunkhouse.

Herders close enough to walk in, or ride if they had a horse, would come and get groceries out of the cellar themselves. One such herder was Domingo, a Basque, who could speak very little English. One day he came for groceries. I had made a peach pie for supper and put it on the table to cool. I knew Bud was coming and I wanted something besides plain canned peaches.

I went to the river to fish and as I passed the Hannah cabin, I saw that Dick and Harve were there. Harve was shoeing his saddle horse. I never gave another thought about the pie. I knew I only had an hour to fish before time to head back to the house.

When I came back to the kitchen the first thing I saw was the pie and it had been cut into. I was furious. Domingo was just coming out of the cellar with a couple of cans of milk.

I was mad as ever at whoever had cut into the pie. I knew Domingo hadn't, but I was raving and ranting 'round the kitchen and Domingo was too scared to move. He looked like he'd seen a ghost. He desperately wanted to leave but was afraid to pass by me and I wasn't paying much attention to him. About then the door opened and Bud walked in. I hadn't even heard him drive in. He could talk to Domingo and, through gestures and broken dialogue, got him out of the kitchen and on the way back to camp.

I learned later that Dick and Harve had gone into the kitchen for a cup of coffee, had seen the pie and had cut themselves a piece. After they'd drunk their coffee, they went back to work.

Domingo was scared to death of me from then on. I tried to apologize to him but I never could make him understand. It wasn't very long ago that I asked Bud if he could remember any unusual incident that happened and that was the first thing he mentioned. Poor Domingo. He must have suffered terribly when lambing and shearing time came and he had to spend a few weeks at Kirkwood.

CHRISTIAN BROTHERS?

Before the road snowed in, Bud asked me if I would make some of my mincemeat for the ranch. I said sure but he would have to get some special ingredients. I pointed out that someone would have to go hunting and get a deer. So, before Bud went to town, I made out a list of just what I would need that we didn't have. Dick and Harve heard the discussion and the wheels of deception began turning in their heads.

While Bud was outside gathering up some things he wanted to take out with him, Dick and Harve told me to tell Bud to buy Christian Brothers brandy only. I knew they were up to no good, but I went along with them. When Bud came in I took the list back and added the brandy, saying, be sure it is Christian Brothers, as that is the secret of my mincemeat.

So off he went. Then I was filled in as to what was going to happen. Dick and I went out to Slate Creek, got my pressure canner, jars, and rings and then headed for White Bird. There we bought the cheapest bottle of brandy the liquor store had, probably $1.50, and headed back for the river.

Several days later when Bud came, sure enough, he had everything I had ordered. I let the brandy sit on the kitchen cupboard, and he asked if he could have a drink of it before dinner. I said sure. After all, he bought it. He said he'd never tasted it before.

As soon as Bud had gone to the bunkhouse, I grabbed a pan and the brandy, and headed for the bedroom. I opened the brandy and poured it into the pan. Then I poured the cheap bottle of brandy we had bought into the Christian Brothers bottle and the good stuff into the cheap bottle. Back downstairs, I set the bottle on the cupboard again.

I got busy and finished dinner. Bud came in before the other guys and I poured him a juice glass of the brandy he thought he had bought.

He took one swallow and said, "Ugh, how can anybody drink this stuff," and I said I didn't know. When you put it in a pie the alcohol cooked out and just left the flavor,

155

that's all I knew about it.

The good bottle of brandy lasted all winter and when we left in the spring we gave the rest to Harve. I'm sure he enjoyed it as he headed out through the Seven Devil's Mountains toward summer camp.

The cheap brandy was left in Bud's room.

Maybe there wasn't always a joke of some kind going on, but if there was any excuse for one, you can bet your bottom dollar someone thought of it.

THE BIG ONE

I remember the day Pick Ward gave me a deep sea rod and reel. He told me this kind of outfit is what I would need to catch the big sturgeon. I used a 120-pound test line and a two-inch barbless hook. And with that, I caught the big one. It was 8 feet, 4 inches and weighed 125 pounds.

I had a hard time getting Dick to come help me get it up from the lower boat landing. He laughed when I told him I had caught a fish bigger than I was. When I finally convinced him it was true, he went with me across the bridge over Kirkwood Creek to the pasture gate and looked down the hay field. Sure enough, I had a big one.

I had left the hook in its mouth and tied it to a hackberry tree to go for help. We had just hoisted it up into the tree by the house and were admiring my catch when Bud drove in. The first thing he said was that he would go out to Nyssa and bring in some friends to have a fish feed.

Now, I wasn't too keen on that idea. We needed that fish for the ones on the ranch, not someone who didn't work there. Dick and Harve dressed it out, we cut it into pieces and put all we could into the refrigerator. Bud took off right away, not wasting any time getting back home. But the more we thought about it the less the idea set with us. After all, whose fish was it?

We had to have a plan to save the sturgeon just for the ranch. I took the ice cube trays out of the freezing compartment of the refrigerator and carefully cut and wrapped enough sturgeon meat to fill the compartment full. When it froze solid you couldn't get it out with an axe. Then we wrapped the rest of the sturgeon in a mantee, loaded it into our jeep, and headed for Slate Creek.

At home we cut and wrapped the fish, marked it, and put it in our freezer. Later we would make several trips to bring in the fish so that all who worked on the ranch had a big feed.

We stayed at Slate Creek overnight and didn't return until late the next day. We wanted to give Bud plenty of time to treat his guests to a sturgeon feed. We found out later that he tried and tried to get the fish out of the freezer unit, and finally had to give up.

He and his friends went back to Nyssa. Bud wasn't too happy with what had happened. But don't think he didn't get even with us in one way or another, except he didn't really know he was doing it.

Between packing hay and grain and extra supplies to Sheep Creek, Dick and Harve were busy keeping their pack strings well shod. All stock was sharp shod in the winter. One time Dick packed some supplies to Domingo's camp. Domingo must have had a bad day because, as Dick rode up, he said, "I quit."

He took off his cap, threw it on the ground and stomped on it, saying, "I quit."

As Dick turned to ride off, Domingo yelled at him again "I quit. Two sheep go up one canyon, one sheep go up two canyon. I quit."

At that Dick roared with laughter and continued on his way. He could hear Domingo for a long ways. Whatever had been the matter, he did quit. He put his personal belongings in his backpack, walked 17 miles to the

157

highway, then went on down the country.

Dick didn't go back for a few days and so knew nothing about his leaving. When he did go back the dogs had gotten into the grub boxes and had literally torn up the camp. Sheep were scattered everywhere.

Sometimes when Dick was going up to Sheep Creek and Bud was there, I'd have Bud boat me up to Sheep Creek so I could go fishing. That was one of the best places on the river. Bud agreed but, like always, there was a catch to it. If he boated me up, I had to pull all the sand burrs and other noxious weeds from the sand bar and along the river. That was a chore, to have to run back and forth every time the bell on the end of the rod rang, signaling a bite. I always anchored my rod solidly to a hackberry or rock when I fished. I wasn't planning on getting dragged into the river by some big sturgeon. I was a cautious fisherman.

There were four left-handed shearers on the shearing crew. They were Larry Garner, Russell Cooper, Don Leeper and Bill Dorman. Bill owned the shearing outfit. The power was furnished by a Kohler gas plant brought in for the work. I never had the time to leave the kitchen long enough to go watch and there was so much activity Dick did not think it was the proper place for me to be. I got to see the bummer lambs as they were brought to a pen near the house to be fed and cared for.

Every now and then I would get in a hurry with my work and have a glorious flop. One in particular was when I was making filling for the cream pies. I was sure they would set if they were put in the refrigerator. When I went to cut them, I didn't say a word to the fellows. I set the pies on the table with cereal bowls next to them. There was plenty of comment about the bowls until they tried to get a piece of pie out of the tin. Then there was no need of explanation. That wasn't the only failure, but that was one of the most embarrassing.

I worked as hard as any man on the outfit, but I'm sure there wasn't a one of them who thought so. If the weather was bad, all you could hear was how lucky I was to be in the house all the time. I wonder how they thought the meals and work were done and by whom.

One morning a friend of ours boated up the river and stopped in to see how things were going. As he left he asked if there was anything I needed.

I said, "Sure, a sturgeon."

He said, okay, he'd bring one to me. I knew he was kidding so I went about my business. A few hours later I heard someone holler to me that he wanted to borrow the jeep. Wasn't long until here came our friend and, sure enough, with a sturgeon.

Seems that he boated up the river and had seen some fishermen on a sand bar. They had just caught a nice, big fish. They had pulled it in to look it over and for some reason or other they thought my friend was a game warden. They said they just wanted to take some pictures before they turned it loose. It was a legal size to keep, but evidently they didn't know that.

So after the picture taking, they started to push it back into the water. Our friend offered to boat it out into the deep water and turn it loose. Of course, he never did turn it loose, he floated it to Kirkwood and gave it to me.

Dick and Harve immediately dressed it out and we had plenty of good eating for quite some time. We were tired of the mutton we'd been eating, so it was a great treat. I often wondered if the men ever figured out they had given up a legal-sized sturgeon. You can bet we never told anyone. Until now, that is. That was quite a number of years ago.

THE CANYON OF THE SNAKE

Where lonely sunsets flare and flame above the canyon rim
While far below the granite walls in darkness fade and dim
Where the rapids run, the dying sun ten thousand diamonds fling
And across the sky the grey geese fly — and tell of coming spring.

On the darkening trail the coyotes wail and a packer makes his way
Toward a lighted lamp in a waiting camp, to a loving place to stay.
Here on Kirkwood Bar they found their star and from the river take
Her richness in grass and salmon — in gold ore and placer flake.

And if these fail they will not wail — this packer and his wife
For from this land — earth, rock and sand — they took full measure
    of life.
They had the sunsets gold and stories told around many a dying fire
The waterfalls jewel and sturdy mule and a horse that will not tire.

Yes all of this and greater bliss — the love of man and wife
As they made their way, day by day, through a rocky but happy life.
Yes they own this land, as much as anyone can, for Heaven was theirs
    to take
From the mile high rim to the river dim — in the canyon of the Snake.

— *Robert L. "Wildhorse" Wiester*

TIGHT SQUEEZE

I think it was about May when we made a trip to Saw
Pit Saddle, then south along the face of the canyon and
down to the river near Brush Creek. Once we got to the
River we returned north to Kirkwood. Just exactly what
the crew was doing I have forgotten, but I suppose they
were tagging sheep or gathering strays missed on the trip
downriver for shearing. I only remember parts of it, but

160

these parts are outstanding in my memory. It was high water month, I know.

There were about ten men. Dick and I had taken in a complete camp for these ten men. I remember being at a place where there was a temporary fenced-in corral. Morris Kohlhepp had been out on vacation. His wife, Dorothy, drove him back as far as Cow Creek Saddle, and he walked the rest of the way. He was all dressed up when he reached the place where the men were working. He just tossed his nice city jacket on the ground and, with white shirt on, climbed over the fence and went to work. I stood in the tent and watched him.

We were gone about two weeks and moved camp several times. At most camps, Dick had to take a mule and pack two ten-gallon cans of water from Gill's Cow Camp every other day. Water was used sparingly. When Bud finally came in he brought another man with him to do the packing. This packer had never been on the river, but Bud needed Dick to help elsewhere.

Coming down off the top we ended up getting off our horses and sliding down a narrow, rocky draw to the river trail above Granite Creek. Then we trailed up the river to Brush Creek where we set up our camp.

Brush Creek was a wonderful place to camp. Lots of nice big pine trees. We stayed here for several days. It was quite a ways up from the river, a nice bar. The packer packed the water up from Brush Creek for camp use. Now we could be a little extravagant. This was really the best part of the trip. I have been back to Brush Creek Camp a few times since and it is always the same as the first time I was there. That area hasn't changed.

When time came to move camp downriver to Sheep Creek, the packer caught and saddled the pack string. I did all the cargoeing of the camp kitchen. When it was done, I got on my horse and headed for the next camp.

Like I said, it was high water time, and going through the "Tight Squeeze" could give you a thrill, even if you weren't looking for one. It wasn't easy pulling your feet out of the stirrups, laying down on your horse's neck, and crowding the rock wall as close as possible to get through. Coming in on the high trail hadn't given the hired packer any idea of what the river trail was like. It could be scary.

The Snake River was high and still muddy. The horses would sometimes have to swim. The last pack mule in the string usually ended up way out in the river swimming for the trail. As I rode down the trail I kept a lookout for the packer and the string to show up behind me whenever I could see far enough back.

When I knew enough time had lapsed for him to catch

"Tight Squeeze." Before the dams were built, this area of the trail was flooded during high water times. This picture, donated by Clark H. Neeley, shows a pack string going through the Tight Squeeze during normal water levels.

Sheep Creek House. Ace Barton and his mother, Lenore Wilson, lived in this house until the early 50s.

up with me, I backtracked and found him stopped on the other side of the Tight Squeeze. When I rode back through, he jumped off his horse and said he needed to check the packs. Good idea.

I waited and, when all packs were checked, I started through again. It really was a scary place the first time you rode it. When I looked back, he hadn't come through. I went back and this time I was getting mad, as I had a dinner to cook at Sheep Creek, ten miles down the country. I needed the supplies that were on the pack mules. I finally took the rope and led the mules through myself. Then, after he rode through, I handed him the lead rope and continued down the trail

When Bud got to Sheep Creek, he took the packer back to town and put Dick back on the pack string. I realize I should have done it all myself in the first place. It takes more than one trip on the trail to get used to it. When we finally got back to Kirkwood, Dick quit and we loaded up and went to Slate Creek.

Morris Kohlhepp and Del Catron were two of the herders who had worked for the Jordans and continued to work for Bud. Morris had his own pack string and moved his own camp. Morris and his wife Dorothy were at Granite Creek.

A stack of horns. These are the horns picked up by Ace Barton along the Snake River and stacked at his home on Sheep Creek. (Photo donated by Clark H. Neeley)

Morris Kohlhepp, packer and herder, about 1948 or 1949.

Henry Bowen's camp was always somewhere between Sheep Creek and Granite Creek. He was always at the upper end of the range closer to Morris's camp.

I remember going to Henry Bowen's camp one day and as we crossed a creek, his dogs splashed through without drinking like the horses did. When we got to camp, Henry went back down to the creek with the two water buckets, filled them and packed them up to camp. He set one pail on the ground so his dogs could drink. Dick asked Henry why the dogs hadn't drunk when they crossed the creek and he replied, "They were too tired." He confessed he

Jim Russell feeding bummer lambs at Kirkwood.

Kirkwood Creek House and Boat. The log bunkhouse can be seen behind the house. Photo was taken about mid-1950.

166

packed water for the dogs at all his camps. Those lucky dogs. They were sure spoiled. Lots of comical things like that took place. I have a hard time remembering them all.

Jim Russell, along with Morris Kohlhepp, came with the ranch. When Bud bought the ranch from Grace and Len Jordan he bought the two men, too. Jim was one who came and went as he pleased. He was especially pleased when the bunkhouse was completed and he had a nice place to stay.

Jim told me one day of something that he had done a few years after Bud bought the ranch. At that time Bud was haying on Big Bar. It was hard to get help. No one wanted to work in 120-degree weather with plenty of rattlesnakes.

This particular time, Jim was boated up to Big Bar to mow hay. The team of horses were already there. Bud left, telling Jim he would be back in a few days. Jim hooked up the team and started cutting hay. It was Thursday, the day the mail boat came up the river. When Jim saw the mail boat, he got the bright idea it would be better to go to Lewiston than work in the hot sun. He unhooked the team, left them in the hay field, and hailed the boat when it came back down the river.

When Bud came a few days later, he was shocked to see the horses had trampled the hay, ruining it all. That was about the end of haying at Kirkwood. Later on, Bud hauled in hay, grain, salt and dog food.

Jim was a very kind old man, and I was very fond of him. He liked me and didn't think Dick treated me very well. He had given me a pair of rawhide hobbles for my use, and one day he noticed that Dick had them tied on his saddle. He went right over to Dick, untied the hobbles, walked over to where I was sitting on my horse and handed them to me. He never said a word to Dick. I was pleased as punch. Dick later took them back, saying I

Sheep Camp on Johnson Bar. I took this picture during the time I was cleaning trail with a garden rake from Sheep Creek to Johnson Bar.

A Camp Tender is shoeing a mule at Warm Springs. (Photo donated by Clark H. Neeley)

A herder just back from shipping lambs at New Meadows

Roaching a mule's tail. Photo taken at Granite Creek.
(Donated by Clark H. Neeley)

Herder Henry Bowen and his dog. (Photo donated by Clark H. Neeley)

Bud Wilson and his Sea Scow on the Snake River. (Photo donated by Clark H. Neeley)

didn't need hobbles for my horse. Later he lost them.

BACK TO SLATE CREEK

Each time we spent a winter on the river it was the same and yet it seemed a little different. Sometimes there were new faces and always old friends. The first two or three winters were very cold. Snow laid on until the storm was over and then the sun came out and it would start feeling like spring was close by. After another winter and spring on the Snake River, we planned to stay at home on Slate Creek for a summer. There was plenty to do there if we wanted to do it. A new fence was needed between Large's and us, so Dick made a deal to do the work; they would furnish the material. When that job was finished, Dick and Dale Tipton made a fence deal. We would share expenses, with Dick and I doing the work, and we would have free pasture for our stock.

I didn't do too well on this job. When Dick was using the wire stretcher, I was holding two ends of the barbed wire we had just spliced. When the wire broke I didn't let go fast enough. The wire and barbs tore my gloves then ripped into the palm of my right hand and almost the full length of my little finger. We went to Robie's and Dick whittled a piece of wood, bandaged the wood splint and my finger straight, and we went back to work. No one thought of going to a doctor.

Nothing was too handy for me until the finger healed. I have a lovely scar on my right hand, but I was lucky it never became stiff. My left hand was only burned a little. I must have let go with it first.

I was always the one who seemed to get hurt in some way when we worked together. I always had bumps and bruises from trying to help. Maybe I was accident-prone. Or maybe I was doing work not quite suited to my ability.

171

We saw lots of Pick and Lillie Ward that summer as they visited their trap lines on Slate Creek and downriver to White Bird. Whenever we went to Riggins we always stopped to see them. Pick would tell Dick what a wonderful job he had. He said Dick should think about hiring out as a trapper.

I secretly figured out Pick's talk was making an impression on Dick and that sooner or later he would be trying his hand at a new job. He decided he'd like to have a couple of dogs now that we were going to be home long enough to keep pets. We went to White Bird and got a male and female pup, Airedale and Plotthound cross. We named them Buck and Tillie. About a month later they got into some kind of poison we had out in the tack shed and died. By then we were used to having them so we went back to White Bird to see if there were any more left of the litter. We were lucky and got two more. These, like the others, were called Buck and Tillie.

Another big project Dick wanted to do was rebuild the flume on the upper flat. If we ever needed to grow anything up there it would be nice to have the water. But this time I refused to help in any way. Rattlesnakes and I did not get along.

Things seemed to be happening pretty fast now. Dick shocked me by deciding to join the Masons in Grangeville. He never was very socially minded, and the very idea of having to wear a suit to the meetings was another shocker. His friend, Harry Hagen, had a big hand in this decision, I'm sure.

First getting the dogs, and then the Masons. Nothing was going to shock me after this. I was sure the next move would be to become a trapper.

In the meantime, Dick's folks moved to Boise, so we didn't see much of them. They surprised us on one visit by bringing a small refrigerator. It really was small, a

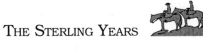

General Electric, the old kind that had the motor on the top. But it was a beauty, and we were grateful. Dick was not one to spend money on something we could get along without.

TRAPPING

Pick kept after Dick about the trapping job. He was wanting to give up the Snake River part of his territory. In time he planned to retire and do some of the things he and Lillie wanted to do.

Dick did hire out to the U.S. Fish and Wildlife Service to trap. Andy Eatmon, of Lewiston, was his supervisor. His wages would be paid for by the Payette National Forest, The Idaho Wool Growers Association, the Idaho Department of Fish and Game, the Idaho Sheep Commission, and the Idaho Fish and Wildlife Service. He would be working for all of these people plus the sheep and cattlemen. This was going to be a new experience but Dick didn't seem to worry about a thing. He just knew he could do it. The first part of the job was working with Pick and Andy packing baits to 1080 (a type of poison) stations.

There was lots of activity now. Dick wanted to make his own boards for fleshing and stretching hides. He was given traps, snares, coyote getters, and anything else needed for the job.

He seemed quite satisfied with this new job. I knew from past experience not to get too involved as nothing lasted very long in this family. I was beginning to accept the fact that everything we did would be short-lived. It took some doing for me to come to that conclusion and stick with it. I knew I had to come to terms with the way of life Dick had chosen for us.

When the work that was to be done on the Salmon River was finished, Dick and I packed up and headed for Kirkwood Creek on the Snake River to trap the winter on Bud's range. We would be living in the Carter Mansion, one mile up the creek from the river where Pick and Lillie had lived when we were building the bunkhouse at Kirkwood.

The Carter house was a mansion only as it related to the wilds of the Snake River. It was marvelous for its time and place, with hardwood floors throughout and lots of windows. Cement porches extended front and back. There was a woodstove, big kitchen cupboards, and a kitchen table with four chairs. The bedroom set included a chest of drawers.

The creek was close enough to make packing water easy. There was some low brush along the creek and the trees were small. The spot was nice and open. Just above the house was a handy place to cross the creek with the jeep. Big flats lay on each side of the house. The front porch was seven or eight feet above the creek.

There was a root cellar out behind the house but I never used it. The outhouse was situated down the creek a ways. We were going to have a great winter.

Pick came and stayed with us and he and Dick put out the trap lines. When they went to Sheep Creek, I went along. We made the Sheep Creek house our headquarters when working on the upper part of the country. We used the Squaw Creek house for a spike camp. It did seem strange, riding past Kirkwood with someone else living there.

It was cold that winter. It didn't make any difference whether you were going up or down the river, the wind seemed to be blowing in your face.

Sheep Creek was a great place to have a winter camp,

peaceful and quiet with a cozy house to live in. Every night the owls would come to the trees around the house and make a chorus of their hooting. We really liked staying there and did so most of the time. It was open as far up the creek as you could see.

The only disadvantage was the long haul uphill from the creek with water. There was a pitcher pump in the house when Bud first got the place, but in a few years it wasn't working because the ditches were not kept up.

Occasionally I could hear a coyote howl and it always made me wonder how long it would be before it got into one of the baits or traps that were out. There were lots of coyotes and bobcats, so trapping was successful on the river. When hides were torn up in such a way you couldn't salvage them, the ears were sent in. I don't think the hides had any value at that time.

After the first run, evenings were spent fleshing and stretching the hides. Also, Dick had to keep a daily diary. It is from this diary that I have copied down all the places he had traps. Some of the places were Stickney Gardens, Lightning Creek, Dry Gulch, Clark's Fork, McGaffee Basin, Sheep Creek, Brownlee's Hole, Royal Gorge, Low Saddle, Hoarhound, Dime Basin, Coyote Basin, Kirby Creek, Cammack Trail, Half Moon, Big Bluff, Kirkwood, Bear Pen, as well as a number of other trails and along the rims. It kept him busy. He trapped bear, coyotes, bobcats and cougar.

Andy came in occasionally to check on things. When the specified time of the month came to mail out Dick's diary, we sent it out by the mail boat. If the date didn't coincide with the mail boat, we rode over the top to Lucile and mailed it. That would mean an overnight stay at Slate Creek. According to the diary we worked every day. This was not a five-days-a-week job.

I started to learn how to set a trap. I practiced for a long time before I could do a good job. Just about everything Dick got involved in ended up with my learning to do the same thing. By spring I didn't do too bad setting a trap, but I didn't catch anything that winter. Still, I enjoyed riding the trap line as winter progressed. Spring was not far away. Towards the end of February, when the lambing and shearing operation was about to begin at Bud's, Dick felt pleased that he didn't have to help. From past experience, he knew how hard they were all going to be working.

It had been seven years since we came to our place on the Salmon River and five years since we made our first trip to the Snake River. We had certainly done a lot of different things and been to quite a few places. It shows we didn't spend too much time at home. But the Snake River was becoming home too. I found that just living one day at a time was better than hoping and planning something that was never going to happen.

When the sheep pulled out for summer range in late May, we packed up and went home. We had a big summer of trapping ahead of us, lots of it in country I had never been in. But Dick knew the country well, having packed for the Payette National Forest many years earlier.

We weren't home long before Dick traded our little red army jeep for a Jeep pickup. He built a rack as high as the cab to haul horses and camp supplies, and, of course, the dogs. They were nearly a year old by then. Dick took them on the trap line with him, training them.

THE SUMMER TRAPPING SCHEDULE

Our summer headquarters was at Squaw Meadows out of McCall. To get there we followed the North Fork of the Payette River past upper Payette Lake and on to a fork in the road. Taking the left-hand fork to the end of the road, we arrived at a nice, one-room log cabin nestled among the trees. A big meadow with a creek meandering through made a picturesque setting. It was ninety miles to Slate Creek and we would travel these roads many times before the summer and fall were over.

Dick and Andy took a camp in first and put up the pasture fence. The posts were already in and the wires lay on the ground. All they had to do was put the wire on a staple that was already driven into the post and another staple on the wire.

Then Dick and I took the camp, supplies, dogs and horses in. We were glad we had the horse trailer now, as it came in handy. Following is a list of the places we traveled according to Dick's diary:

From our headquarters at Squaw Meadows we went horseback to set traps, snares, or coyote getters on Jackson Creek, Elk Meadows, French Creek, Bear Pete Ridge, Hazard Lake, Clayburn Creek, Victor Creek, Twenty Mile, Lava Ridge, and Little French Creek. Since I do not have the full summer months' diaries, I'm sure there are many I have missed.

By Jeep we traveled in the Marshall Mountain area and the Brundage Mountain area from Squaw Meadows over Sesesh Summit to Burgdorf and on to the War Eagle Mine area, the Elk Lake area, Carey Dome, Beartrap Saddle, Golden Anchor Mine and places in between. Several bands of sheep made this area their summer range.

We also had Meadows Valley, Little Salmon, and the Big Salmon. Other places were Race Creek, Rapid River, John Day Creek, Wick's Ranch, Hagen Range above White Bird, Joseph Plains, the Boles area, the Lucile area, and up Slate Creek, Little Slate, North Fork Slate Creek, Telephone Ridge, Dead Horse Ridge, Robie Ranch, Fiddle Creek, Big Canyon and the Spencer Ranch.

According to the mileage recorded, we traveled about

2,000 miles by Jeep alone each month. There is no way of knowing how many miles we traveled by horseback. There were very few days in the six months of diaries I have that show we were not on the road going some place. We did go to the Hunter's Conference held in Stanley Basin. We went in style. We flew in.

On the first trips into any new country, we set all the traps, put out the snares, and placed the getters. Before time to go back to the Snake River for the winter we made many trips to check these stations. The summer passed quickly.

I was doing better at setting traps, although I only caught one cat during the summer. I remember one time I set the trap and did everything just right and on the next trip into the Marshall Mountain area, as we rounded a curve, I could see someone at the trap I had set. It was the fellow who was staying at the lookout at Carey Dome. He was taking the cat out of the trap. By the time we got to the spot, he was going up the road fast, dragging my cat. The hides were no good, but I wanted to take it out myself. It was the first one I had caught. I would have gone up to the lookout and confronted the guy, but Dick wouldn't let me.

When fall came and it was time to leave, we took down the pasture fence, cleaned the cabin, left a supply of wood in the woodbox, packed everything up and loaded the horses. We were on our way back to Slate Creek.

Dick got into the preparation of the bait horses that year. The previous year it had all been done by the time he hired on. We went to Lewiston for three days while that was being done and then hauled the baits to a special box Dick had built in the shed to store them safely. He was also busy putting out the 1080 stations, some by horseback, some by Jeep. It was after Christmas before we went to the Snake River.

WINTER TRAPPING

Again we were at the Carter Mansion. Everything was just as we had left it. We had our upriver camp at Sheep Creek with a spike camp at Squaw Creek.

The work was easier that winter and I went with Dick on every trip possible. Still, there were times when I had to stay at home to do washing or ironing. At Sheep Creek I used the washboard but went down to the Kirkwood house to use the washing machine when we were at the Carter house. I would bring the clothes back to hang them so I could take care of them as they dried and not have to make another trip down the creek to get them. I thought it was very good for Bud to let me use the machine.

On one such washing trip to Kirkwood, things didn't work out like they were supposed to. Dick and I packed our clothes on mules. On this particular day, I had just loaded the wet clothes into the pack boxes and started across the creek when something spooked the mules. Away they went. I hadn't put the mantees on the boxes and so there were no tops. Those darn mules bucked and jumped and ran all over the flat, scattering clothes along the way. When we had finally caught all of them and got the clothes picked up, I was fit to be tied. If I'd had a gun we would have had some dead mules. We finally got back to the Carter House and I just went to the creek, rinsed out the clothes and hung them on the line dripping wet.

Trapping was much like it had been the winter before. When the weather warmed up we would take cans of tomatoes and put them in one of the little creeks along the trail, covering them so the sun never hit them. When we came back down the trail we would have a nice, cold can of tomatoes for lunch. They were a great thirst quencher.

I don't remember seeing many rattlesnakes along the

trail. The vibration of the stock would scare them away before we got to them. It was more likely to see them higher up off the river trail.

When spring really arrived, the flowers began to appear along the trail. Many times I saw anemones come up in the middle of a hard-packed trail. It was amazing. There was Indian paintbrush that grew near Granite Creek that was the tallest and darkest red I had ever seen. The hillsides were dotted with flowering pear cactus and there were many other wildflowers I didn't know the names of.

That winter Dick and the dogs treed six cougars. One was a trophy hide measuring nine feet. Before the winter was over his count was approximately 150 predators caught, treed, or killed outright.

Some traps were pulled and taken to another spot when it was apparent that no sign of cat or coyote was in the area. It was constant work. We tried to make the rounds to visit every setting at least every eight days. Longer than that could cause problems.

The dogs were getting real good at tracking. They liked it and would get excited. This behavior was catching. Sometimes it was too exciting for me when I'd find myself in a place I wished I hadn't.

When spring came and it was time to pull out for summer range of trapping, all traps, snares and getters were gathered. All 1080 baits were picked up and destroyed. It took as long to gather them up as it did to put them out.

Before this winter was over, I had the required number of bobcat hides to make a fur coat. Since I had seen the coat Dorothy Taylor had many years ago, I thought this would be the time for me to have one. Dick said if I wanted one I would have to set my own traps, do the stretching and fleshing myself. He wanted no part of it. So that is just what I did. We sent the ears in for count. Later that summer I took the hides to the Lewiston Fur Shop and had a coat made. It took ten hides and I had one extra for repairs if needed.

This trapping job lasted for almost three years. I wasn't surprised when Dick was less thrilled about trapping than in the beginning. I was more surprised he stayed with it as long as he did. We were two winters on the Snake River and two full summers and late falls. Then, instead of going back to the Snake River the next January, Dick quit and again went to work for Earl McNutt Construction. He signed for the same job as before, night work.

The trapping job was exciting and a great learning experience while it lasted, and I ended up with a fur coat, so it wasn't all wasted time. Dick learned many things too, and we did a lot of traveling. Maybe he was tired of traveling.

SLATE CREEK WASHOUT — 1959

Dick quit the trapping job on January 10th. Two days later he hired out to McNutt Construction, driving a Euclid dump truck. This time the road work was between John Day Creek and Slate Creek. He would have the graveyard shift again.

It was cold that month. According to a Hallmark datebook I found among my souvenirs, temperatures ranged from zero to 46 degrees. Snow fell many times. Dick decided, since it was too cold to work outside, he would do some work inside on the house. He ordered tongue and groove knotty pine for the ceiling and two ceiling lights to place between the log beams at the kitchen end of the room. Don Caward of Riggins did the electrical work. The REA would put in a two-phase line when the required wiring was finished.

Enough lumber was purchased also to put a ceiling in the shed so, along with the new attic in the house, there would be more storage space.

Before the end of January the long-awaited fur coat arrived from the Lewiston fur shop. For four days the temperature hung at 16 degrees above zero, but the day the coat arrived it had moderated to 46 degrees. I had to wear the coat some place, regardless, so Dick drove me to Riggins to show it off. It was a beauty. It is still a beautiful coat, 34 years old and just like new.

We talked some about planting another garden that

spring. With the flume repaired and in good condition now, we would have lots of gravity water from the creek.

There were so many things I wanted done in the house now that the ceiling was in. The logs out in the field really bothered me. I wondered if anything was ever going to be done with them.

The Lynx Coat. Bonnie is shown at Slate Creek modeling her new lynx coat. Note the fence has been built and roses planted.

Dick built the dogs a fancy log duplex with a large fenced yard so they would have plenty of space for exercise. He took real good care of his dogs.

One weekend a friend of Dick's came and asked him if he could take Dick's dogs up Fiddle Creek, as he was having cougar problems. After Dick spotted the cougar and gave the signal for the chase, the dogs really got excited. They hadn't been on a hunt for a long time. Dick kept up with them on horseback, and when it was getting too dark for him to continue the chase, the dogs were too far ahead to hear his whistle to come back. Dick rode back to the pickup and came home.

The next morning, Sunday, he took his horse and went looking for the dogs. He rode all day, calling and whistling, but they were not to be found. Several days later they came in on their own, tired, hungry, and foot-sore. They were glad to be home and we were glad to know that if they were lost they knew how to find their way back. Dick had trapped all through that country so they knew their way around.

I was busy with leather orders on the side. There was always plenty to do. The coldest part of the winter was behind us and we were looking forward to spring. We ordered garden seed and prepared to plant. I guess life was going too good because, just when we thought nothing could go wrong, it did.

The weather moderated quickly causing a mud slide way up the creek. It blocked the creek flow long enough to build up pressure and when it broke loose it took everything in its path that was loose. And then some. By the time it got to our place it took three-fourths of the upper flat. What a horrible sight. This place seemed like the jinx for us. Again we would have to have Ted Taknen from Old Meadows come with his dozer to repair the damage.

There was a good-sized island across the creek from the upper flat. Some time in the past, high water had made a detour of the creek and a small stream of water split off and flowed on the far side of the island. Ted decided the only thing to do was use the island for a fill. It contained tall cottonwoods, birch, alder and willow trees, as well as brush. Ted rechanneled the creek by moving the island, trees, rocks, and mud. When the fill was completed we had a very large piece of ground. We were amazed.

Stakes were driven at the edge of the original solid ground so that we would know where the good ground ended and the fill began. Nothing too substantial could be built on this ground because in time the trees would rot and the ground would sink in some places.

The creek had a pretty straight course now. Ted said that eventually, over the years, it could return to its original channel. We figured that would be too far in the future to worry about and hoped that this would be the last of the dozer work.

I really loved living along the creek but now I worried during storms, what would come next? What a year so far, and just as things were going along so well.

It was amazing the amount of work Dick could do along with his night job. Nothing was too tough for him if he wanted to do it. He decided to build a hay barn. He needed a place for hay, grain and shelter for the horses. He built a frame of 2 x 4s. Nailing the sides together on the ground, he used the Jeep truck and ropes to raise each side, then nailed it in place. It turned out to be a very good structure.

We let the pasture grow and when it was ready to cut we were both out in the field with hand scythes cutting. We stacked and eventually pitched the grass hay onto an old mantee and drug it to the barn with the Jeep and Dick pitched it, forkful by forkful, into his new barn. He really worked harder than he should have.

In September I joined Eastern Star in Grangeville. I thought we would be staying on the creek now. Traveling days were over. The horses, mules and dogs were all doing well.

I put the word out to a car salesman in Grangeville that I wanted to buy a good used car. Dick said I could, but would have to pay all the expenses myself. I figured with my leatherwork I could swing it. A car was found, but I only had five dollars on me so that became the down payment. I now owed $345 on a Chevy coupe. I had a month to make $120, the balance of the down payment.

So I now had to get busy and make more leather articles to raise money for the license, gas and whatever you need when you buy a car. Also, I got a job on Sundays tending bar at Summerville's in Riggins and working in the restaurant whenever needed. Then there was the balance of monthly payments I had to make. It wasn't much, but when Dick said I had to pay for everything myself, he meant it!

When my grandmother died I received $500 from her estate. I used it to buy furniture, including a white divan, two end tables, a coffee table, and a tangerine-colored chair. Dick insisted on picking out the colors. It looked great in the log house. Was I ever proud of this new furniture.

Andy Eatman and a friend came from Lewiston and gathered all the traps and gear Dick had used for trapping. Now that the bait box was out of the shed, we had more room for other things. He built a workbench for making pack saddles and repairing equipment. He kept these things up, though he was not using them at the moment.

Even though Dick worked the night shift, he became used to the hours. I had to more or less keep daylight hours as there were things that had to be taken care of during the day. But we made new friends with people who worked on the construction job, so we enjoyed more social life.

When fall came and hunting season began, McNutt's shut down to give the men a chance to hunt. Dick and Dale Tipton went up Slate Creek, taking the horses and mules, their camp dogs, and all other necessities.

They had only been gone four days when word reached Dale's wife and me that a close friend had passed away and the funeral was in two days. Addie and I talked it over and decided maybe we'd better go to camp and tell the guys, as they would want to go to the funeral.

We started out early in the morning with Addie driving. When we came to the pickup and horse trailers we knew we had reached the right trail to take to their camp.

It was probably four or five miles uphill; we crossed Slate Creek and started up the trail on foot. Addie wasn't what you'd call a hiker, but she figured she could make it slowly, with plenty of rest stops. We hadn't gotten half way when she decided she just couldn't make it. She was a heavy girl, and of course I was well broken in for walking trails, although most of the time I rode my horse.

Finally I saw that time was going faster than we were, so I told her to sit down on a log and I'd go ahead to camp and send a horse back for her.

I started out at a good clip and made good time. I topped out in a clearing and to my surprise Dick had set a coyote trap alongside the trail and he had caught a coyote. I got the idea right then and there that it sure would be great to be dragging a dead coyote into their camp. It wasn't the best spot to corner the animal, but I figured if I got a stick long enough I could whack it on the end of its nose and stun it enough so that I could throw it on the ground and stomp on the rib cage to kill it. Trapping experience was going to pay off. The only trouble was it had the range of a full circle. I didn't want to get too close, and couldn't find a stick long enough. I tried and tried but finally gave up. I thought of Addie sitting down the trail scared to death so I gave up my quest to become the noble hunter and went on to camp. The fellows had just gotten in and were they ever surprised to see me. They hadn't unsaddled yet so Dale took Dick's horse and went after his wife.

We stayed in camp all night. Since they were coming out the next day anyway, we could have saved ourselves all that long walk by just staying home. Then, after all, the guys said they didn't want to go to the funeral since they had their meat to take care of. It was all kinda' exciting, anyway.

That week off from work went by fast and work started again. Just before Thanksgiving, Dick and I went to town for groceries, town being Grangeville, and Dick went on his buying spree.

Sometimes I really hated to go grocery shopping with Dick. He was a compulsive shopper. He liked to buy groceries and bought as if he were feeding a family of six or more. He wanted to make sure he never ran out of anything. He wasn't that big an eater either, just liked to possess it all. Maybe sometime in his early years he had gotten short of food and this way he was sure he always had plenty.

We had Thanksgiving that year at the Tiptons at Slate Creek. Christmas was at our house, open to friends. All in all this year had not been too bad, except for the slide. Dick had a good job to pay for the dozer work and seemed to be coping with it. How long it would last was anybody's guess. I think he planned on staying until the job ended, although I never talked to him about it. Some things were getting done around the place, and that was the main thing I guess.

NEW HOUSE

Days were routine and nothing much was done, outside. Lots of work was planned for later on, though. Because of the night job, mornings were for sleeping but Dick decided to see how much he could get done during the afternoons.

He was obsessed with the new piece of land we had acquired as a result of the flood and dozer work. He kept talking about building another log house on it. I had no idea what was in his mind.

Along towards spring he suggested we make a trip to Boise to visit his parents. Not too far down the highway I realized what this trip was all about. He began saying what a great place Slate Creek would be for his folks. At that time they were renting a place, and Dick's plan was to build a new house for us on the upper flat and let his folks have our house. They could do what they wanted with it.

I couldn't see building another house when we hadn't finished the one we were living in, but he had his mind set on this project so I resigned myself to it. There was nothing I could do about it anyway.

This visit was painful for me and I couldn't wait for it to end. Before we left Boise, plans were made for his folks to move to Slate Creek. Dick was elated. He always wanted to do something special for his folks and he figured this would be his crowning glory.

When we returned home, Dick spent the afternoons while he was working for McNutt figuring out just where the house should be built and how. It would have to be set on the original solid ground, not on the fill.

The first log would be set into the poured foundation. When the cement set, the solid cement floor would be poured. This would be easier than waiting until all the logs were up. He could then continue putting up the rest of the logs and marking the openings for the doors and windows. This being summer, he figured this was the best time to build.

I couldn't seem to get too interested in this new house; I felt cheated in a way. The logs to be skidded to the upper flat to build a new house should have been used for our existing house. I was hoping he would change his mind and let his folks have the big space at the upper end of the place. I think he was obsessed with the idea of building another log house. He really like to work with logs and an axe. I knew there were some things I would always have to do whether I wanted to or not.

It took several trips to Grangeville to gather the materials needed to begin work. We skidded the logs to the upper flat with the Jeep pickup. Now we were ready to start. Other than myself, Dick had no one to help him. This building would be the same size as the first one, 20 feet by 30 feet on the inside.

We worked every day, now that he was not on the road job. Soon I found myself spending my days sitting on a log with a draw knife, taking off bark. This time Dick built saw horses to hold the logs so that I could sit on a log with my feet on the ground. This was a lot easier for me than climbing up on the last log. We both stripped bark until we had several logs ready, then he would start notching the logs and I'd continue stripping.

I would have to stop stripping long enough to help him

191

cross-haul the next log into place. The upper log over the doors and windows was done in the same manner as we had done the Kirkwood bunkhouse. The logs would have to stand several months to settle and the sheathing and roof would come later. Having the floor poured made cleaning up the wood chips an easier job. We were really learning a lot about how to build a log house.

We had done what work we could on the new house when a friend of ours, Speck Anscomb, brought us his cow that was going to calve. He had moved and had no place to keep her. Speck owned a bar in Cambridge. Soon after the calf was born, Speck broke his leg and needed a bartender. It was only for a month, so Dick decided to go. We took our camp and moved to Cambridge. We had to take the dogs, too, as we couldn't leave them that long. We hauled the cow and calf Speck had given us in the horse trailer and Dick repaired fence to hold them.

The holidays came and went. More than a year had passed since the trip to Boise when the big move was planned and Dick felt it was time to finish what had been started. There was a big rush to get things done. He had begun breaking a few horses when the weather moderated.

Dick's folks had gotten us two extra-large plate glass doors at an auction house in Boise for just a few dollars. They were much too big for a door in a house, so Dick cut his openings in the house so he would be able to cut the doors to fit. We then had to order one door that would be used for the back of the house. Window openings had been measured to his specifications and we went to Grangeville to order them made.

After the logs had settled, Dick finished the upstairs of the house with lumber, as we hadn't cut enough logs for a two-story house. The rafters, sheathing, and roof of tar paper went on. The work on the inside was now in progress. The upstairs was floored and partitioned into two rooms, one east and one west with the stairwell in the center.

On each side of the east bedroom, along the north and along the south, Dick cut a portion of the wallboard out for access to storage under the slope of the roof. The wallboard was replaced with special clamps to finish off the wall. That way, there was no swinging door. A large plate glass door was put in the east wall for good ventilation. Since there were no outside stairs, no one could walk out the door. It was a long way to the ground. We then went to the outside of the house and chinked the spaces between the logs. Next was building a cinderblock chimney on the west side of the house. Dick had cut openings for windows on each side of the chimney. When the windows and doors arrived, they were installed. It was beginning to look like a house, inside and out.

The downstairs was partitioned off into four rooms. The kitchen and living room were all one room, 20 feet by 15 feet. The storeroom was probably 12 feet by 15 feet and the cellar took up the remainder of that section. There was ample space for everything.

A door was put in between the kitchen and storeroom. The windows used in the west bedroom were from a yard sale we had gone to in Boise.

When all this was finished, we hired Smoky Ruttman of White Bird to come and build the kitchen cupboards, counter, and an island in the center to separate the rooms. Jay McCulley had loaned me his electric stove and that was fitted into the island. This counter island was about eight feet long, nice and handy.

We still had the wood cookstove and we put it in the storeroom. One day, a few years later, we came home to find the electric stove had been taken out and there was just an empty space remaining. We moved the island into the storeroom, set the woodstove in its place, and went on from there. We had known that some day Jay would need the stove back, but it was a shock to have it gone. I had really become attached to it.

The following spring we ordered 26 Lombardy poplar trees to be planted on the west side of the house. What a job to pack water to all of them to keep them alive. Next we ordered a red-leaf maple and a mountain ash. At that time I also ordered a climbing blaze rose and planted it to climb the cinderblock chimney. It grew to be a beautiful plant.

In time we set out two blue spruce, one on each side of the lean-to porch on the front of the house. All these things were nice, until it came time to pack water. Guess who was usually the only one around? It took bucket after bucket to keep them alive. Most of the poplars finally died out.

We now took time off to go to Cedars and cut some cedar blocks for shakes to re-roof the first house and enough for the new house. This shake project would probably be done next year.

An enormous amount of work had been done this past year, some of it not planned in the beginning. We were both worn out and it was a relief when fall came. The big move would take place next spring. What we needed now was a vacation. When hunting season came along, we hired out to Larry Garner again to pack hunters. We would be in the Big Creek country at the Jess Taylor ranch once more.

AT JESS TAYLOR'S

Dick went to work again for Larry Garner. We met him in New Meadows and followed him as far into the wilderness as Big Creek. We left the rigs there and went by horseback into the Cold Meadows and Chamberlain Basin area. Russ Cooper from Lucile, Idaho, and another man were helping. After the first of the hunters were packed out to spike camps, Larry had us go to the Jess Taylor ranch, which was down Big Creek, to take care of the hunters wanting to hunt in that area.

I don't know what the arrangements were between Larry and Jess. I know that all the hunters coming in for us to take care of were Larry's and that at times Dick packed some of Jess's hunters also.

We lived in the house across the creek from the Taylors, so we had a good place to cook for hunters until they were packed out to their separate camps.

I particularly liked this place. There were many places across Big Creek that I could explore in the afternoons if I had no one to cook for. Then there were the times I went with Dick to check on the hunters. The weather was wintry, but much more pleasant than this time of year in the higher country. Jess had a very good airstrip on his ranch, making it handy for people to fly in and out.

On one trip up Pioneer Creek, the trail climbed quite a distance from the creek. The dogs were in the lead. Suddenly they stopped and stood looking down the hillside towards the creek. As soon as Dick saw what they were looking at, he called the dogs to him. They didn't bark, just sat and looked.

On top of a huge boulder were two cougar kittens. The mother was standing on her hind legs with fore paws on the upper side of the boulder. Five head of deer were feeding along the creek. We knew the cat was training her young to hunt. We just sat on our horses and watched.

After awhile Dick decided to give the dogs a chance to tree a cougar. We tied up the pack string and took off down the hill towards the cougar. When they heard us, they turned and started running. The deer scattered.

A one-day job. Dick is packing wire for new fencing on White Bird Hill.

Larry Garner's Cold Meadows Hunting Camp. This photo shows the cook tent and tents where the hunters stayed. (Photo by Russell "Bud" Cooper)

Pack String. Russell "Bud" Cooper leaving Cold Meadows camp with the pack string. (Photo donated by Russell "Bud" Cooper)

Dick gave the signal to the dogs to start the chase. By the time we got to the creek we could just barely hear the dogs. They were hot on the trail.

By this time Dick had decided to call the dogs off but they didn't hear him. When I looked back up the mountain to where my horse was, I was wishing I had stayed on top. It was getting late in the afternoon and we still had a long way to go and a camp to set up. The dogs would find their way back down the creek.

This turned out to be an exciting hunting season. Towards the end Ted Trueblood, the famous outdoor writer, came with his camera crew in on a special hunt. He wanted to kill a deer and an elk with a special gun he had brought in, a muzzleloader. This trip would be published in one of the outdoor sports magazines Ted worked for.

We were given some nice pictures of this hunt. He got

Author Ted Trueblood and Dick Sterling with pack string.

both his deer and elk with his muzzleloader. This meant he had to be quite close in order to kill them.

When the season was over we packed back to Cold Meadows and I caught a ride to Slate Creek with some hunters that were going that way. Dick came out later with Larry and all the stock. He drove the pickup home since he had gone hunting the last two days of the season and got our winter's meat.

Ted Trueblood with the deer killed with his muzzleloader.

SPECK

Back at Slate Creek, everything picked up where we left off. I was again part-time at Summerville's. The Christmas holiday was close and we stayed at home. There were so many things to do now that the big move was coming up.

As lambing and shearing was about to start on the Snake River, Dick hired out to help Bud. He didn't expect to be gone more than six weeks and didn't take a saddle horse. I stayed at home with the dogs and kept busy with leatherwork and my part time job.

When Dick returned, we were contacted by some people who wanted to buy a small piece of land along the creek to build a retirement home. Dick sold them a piece of ground at the lower end of the flat that joined Mahurins. This was just the beginning of selling lots.

Move to New House

By then the new house was ready. It didn't take long to move. We didn't own that much. Just before we moved, some people came who wanted to buy my wagon-wheel furniture. I decided to sell it because I discovered I could buy furniture direct from the factory with our store license.

This time we got a davenport, chair, rocker, bookcase, two end tables and a coffee table, all for less than I'd paid

Second house at Slate Creek. The photo shows the yew wood corral and the first house in the background.

for the first furniture. It was also wagon-wheel style, solid white oak and solid walnut. The colors were more subdued. The only piece of that furniture I still have is the coffee table, the last of my grandmother's inheritance.

When our things were out of the old house Dick tore up the subfloor, built a frame around the bottom logs of the house, and poured a solid cement floor and foundation. The addition to the house was finished. When the cement set, the place would be ready for his folks to move in. There were still plenty of things to do to finish the new house.

The summer was a busy one. We poured cement for a large porch in back with a lean-to roof. We bought two more trees, a mountain ash and a red-leafed maple. They were planted in the back yard.

We finally purchased a used Maytag washing machine. Everything worked on it. We also purchased a second chest-type freezer, so now we had two. I would have preferred a pump to bring water from the creek into the house. It never happened.

Later in the summer, Dick and I made a trip to Lewiston to the doctor. On the way back, going up the Culdesac grade, we were hit from behind by a car driven by a lady from Cottonwood. That was almost the end of my car, the one I had worked so hard to buy and keep in good condition. As a result of this accident I had to have knee surgery and was on crutches for months.

CABIN CREEK

When fall came Dick and a friend decided to work for Rex Lanham at a hunting camp at Cabin Creek in the Idaho Primitive Area. Cabin Creek is about five miles up Big Creek from Jess Taylor's. That's where the trail comes down from Cold Meadows. I did not want him to go. With him gone, I would have a hard time packing water and wood and getting up and down stairs. I was angry that he would leave me for two months. I struggled by myself and got no help, no help from anyone, including Dick's folks who were then living in the house below me.

After a month had passed Dick sent word that I was to fly into Cabin Creek with Rex. I decided to take only one crutch with me. It was going to be difficult no matter what. The dog, Tillie, had died and we just had the one, which I left with Dick's dad.

At Cabin Creek we had a cabin to ourselves. When I got there, I realized the reason I was called in. Dick and his friend needed someone to cook for them.

I did nothing for the hunters there, however. They had a very nice cook house and cabins, everything they needed. Mrs. Lanham did their cooking. It was a lovely place and I was glad for the chance to be there. It was easier on me than at home.

When the season was over, Dick, his friend, and I were flown out together. When we were over Slate Creek, Rex buzzed the house where Dick's folks were now living and his dad came to the emergency landing strip along the Salmon River to pick us up. No stock had been taken in for this job.

Dick's friend was taken to White Bird and we settled down for the winter. The year 1960 was nearly over. Things were easier for me. Dick chinked the logs on the inside. The outside was already done. Dick moved the cedar blocks left over from the first roofing job but never got around to making the shakes.

By spring my knee was healing nicely but I still used one crutch and found it difficult to get around outdoors.

Dick decided we needed a root cellar. He dug one along the lane into our house facing it with yew logs. He really did a good job, though I'm not sure we used it all that much.

He also built another yew-wood stockade corral. He tore down one of the original corrals from the lower place and moved it up to where we were. We needed a corral for the horses and mules. A log woodshed was built.

He had acquired another dog. It was a redbone hound. Why he needed a hunting dog, I couldn't imagine. He moved the fancy log duplex doghouse up from the other place and built another fenced-in yard.

For my birthday, Dick had bought me a blue shepherd pup, Speck. She was a cute, smart dog, and strictly mine. I would train her myself with no interference from Dick. I wasn't the best trainer, but I had watched Dick. Everything went fine and she was doing very well. When she was about a year old, I got sick and had to go to the hospital, leaving Dick in charge of Speck.

Well, she wasn't going to mind him in any fashion. I

Dick Sterling at the yew wood cellar at Slate Creek

don't know what she did, but I suppose she wouldn't do what he told her. Anyway, he lost his temper about something, took her up the creek and shot her. I couldn't believe it when I asked where she was. So much for my birthday present. Things were a little cool for awhile, but then you can't go on forever worrying about such things.

There was no prospect of a job in view and Dick decided we would go to the Middle Fork of the Salmon River and camp for the remainder of the summer.

WATERFALL SUMMER

Friends from Craigmont hauled our stock, camp gear, groceries, and other supplies to the little mountain community of Big Creek. We planned to summer on the Middle Fork of the Salmon River where it flows through the Big Horn Crags of the Frank Church River of No Return Wilderness. This is the same general area where Dick worked for Larry Garner. Our camp would be at Waterfall Campground across from the mouth of Big Creek where it flows into Middle Fork. This campground is 27 miles from the nearest road.

This would be a summer of just camping and exploring new country with our dogs. Before we left McCall, we made arrangements with Bob Fogg, bush and mail plane pilot, to drop our mail and anything we might need at Soldier Bar, the closest landing field in that area. We'd been told the mail plane would land and take off on mail day, or any other time we needed the plane, before the sun rose. Going into a new country, we wanted to be sure to have a way of contacting the outside world in case of accident.

We left my car at the airport in McCall in case we needed transportation. It took a long day to get to Big Creek and after the trucks were unloaded and the stock put in the corral, our friends returned to Craigmont. We had supper at the Big Creek cafe, rolled out our bedrolls and called it a day.

The next morning after breakfast we packed the mules and headed down Big Creek. The weather was beautiful and I felt there was nothing more peaceful than to be riding down a trail knowing this was what you'd been dreaming of doing. The dogs were excited to be on the go again. Big Creek was so clear it looked only a few inches deep, but I learned differently after crossing it several times later in the summer. When it came late afternoon we started looking for a good place to camp for the night.

We knew we would be camping out two nights for sure, and maybe more as neither one of us had been down the trail to the mouth. Next morning we packed up again. The day was uneventful and we made camp again the second night. We knew by the country we'd reach our destination the next day.

On the morning of the third day, as we rode down the trail, we realized we were getting closer to the mouth of the creek. A little farther down the trail we saw a sign that read, "Soldier Bar Landing Strip."

We tied the pack string, crossed the creek and climbed the 600-foot trail to the strip. The dirt and grass runway sloped to the west. They called it a one-way, or blind, strip. A pilot had to take off and land from the same direction. It sure looked mighty small to me. This high bench looked like the only one around. A gravestone was located there marking the burial of a U.S. Calvary soldier killed in the Sheepeater War in 1879.

Returning to the creek, we picked up the pack string and continued down the trail, arriving at the mouth of the creek where a pack bridge spanned the Middle Fork of the Salmon River. What a wonderful sight that was. A sign read, "Soldier Bar, Five Miles." We were 27 miles from the Smith Creek/Big Creek trailhead where we started.

We crossed the bridge and the trail began to rise above the river, a steep climb. Then, suddenly, we came to the nicest camp ground you ever saw. Lots of big pines provided plenty of shade. I had no idea such a place could exist. We were thrilled at this place we planned to call our camp for the next three months.

Later, by signs, we discovered that the Waterfall trail was eleven miles from the trailhead and rose 5,000 feet from the river. I never went to the very end of the trail head as it started at Terrace Lakes.

We put up our tent and set our cookstove out in the open. It was a wonderful stove with a big oven and a good-sized cooktop. Unlike the usual sheepherder stove, it came in two pieces, with the oven supported by legs at one end. We had a table, two lawn chairs, and everything for a comfortable camp.

We gathered squaw wood to clean the camp but wood was plentiful. Camp water had to be packed but we were close enough to the creek for it to be easy. I was used to it. Except for Kirkwood and someone else's house, I had always had to pack water.

Dick put hobbles on the bell mare, kept a wrangle horse, and turned the rest loose. After supper we unrolled our bedrolls and retired early. Next morning at daylight we woke up to a sight I had never expected to see. At least twenty bighorn sheep were staring at us from the rim overlooking our campground. When we started to move about they disappeared. We would see them nearly every morning from then on during the three months we were in this camp. We never bothered them, and never saw them anytime during our rides up the trail. But they were there every morning at daylight.

After a few days of getting settled in and getting wood cut, Dick decided the campground needed an outhouse. There was one across the river at the mouth of the creek. It had been built by the Forest Service for use while they built the pack bridge across the river. So Dick took a mule

207

over and packed it across the bridge and up to the campground. He spent several days digging the hole. He was figuring it to be a permanent addition to the site.

When everything in camp was in order, we took a ride up the Waterfall Trail to see what kind of country was above us. We rode every day farther and farther until we ran out of trail. There was no trail down the river from camp. A trail went up river but we had plenty of time to explore that way.

We had other things to do. We had a gold mine up Big Creek. We didn't know where, what drainage, or any-thing, only a general description of what it looked like. We went up every draw, creek, and game trail until, one day, we finally found the right creek. We went as far as we could, but there was a lot of work to do to get near the mine. No one had been on the trail for years. High water had dislodged trees and rocks. For weeks we cleaned and rebuilt the trail and struggled to get to the top of the mountain.

At last we came upon a small, broken-down log cabin and knew we had found the spot. We found the tree with the claim in the tobacco can just like we were told it would be. A large rockslide, too steep for horses, had to be climbed on foot. We switch-backed our way to the top and, sure enough, there was the mine entrance.

It was the best mine tunnel I had ever seen, built into solid rock with a tiny stream of water running through it. We had flashlights and carbide lights on our hats to see as we entered the tunnel. I got spooked and didn't go as far as Dick did, but he sure got excited. I knew he would never do any mining, but at least we had a gold mine. At the price of gold then it wasn't worth messing with.

When we left the mine and the cabin, we covered our trail behind us so it would grow back the way it was when we found it. We never went back to it again. The satisfaction of finding it was enough for Dick. He knew he could find it again if he ever wanted to.

Finding the mine was one of the main reasons Dick wanted to camp at Middle Fork. After that we just stayed around camp, rode the five miles to Soldier Bar to meet the mail plane and enjoyed life in general. Once a couple of Forest Service men from the Bernard Creek Guard Station stopped by, but they never came back again. Guess they thought we were doing okay.

Almost every evening we would saddle up and ride the trail above camp to sit on a point overlooking the Middle Fork. With binoculars we could see mountain goats, mountain sheep, deer, and elk, all from one spot. It was fascinating and always peaceful and quiet. Now and then you could hear woodpeckers and there were three pairs of pileated woodpeckers that stayed near camp. These are big birds and very pretty with their bright red crests. We never had rattlesnakes in camp, but several timber rattlers were seen farther up the trail.

After exploring all the trails close by, we decided it was time to see what was up the river. Without a map we had no idea about the country at all. When we were on the river we saw Don Smith, float outfitter, a couple of times. He was floating down the river in his big raft. At that time I said to myself, "I'll stick to my horse; you can have the raft." We didn't ride up the river every day, but we'd go a little farther each time we went. On one trip we saw a building ahead of us, but we weren't curious enough to continue on that day. Next time we'd find out.

Dick was having a few twinges in his back so he decided he'd better go to town and see a doctor. We rode to Soldier Bar and left a note for Bob Fogg to pick him up on his trip the following week. When the day arrived we went to the landing field, Dick got on the plane, and I took his horse back to camp.

Now I was alone with the dogs, the horses, and the mules. There wasn't anyone for miles but me. At least I hadn't seen anyone. While Dick was in town he met some of our friends who asked where I was. Dick said, "I left her in camp." I guess our friends were mad at him for leaving me alone. They didn't realize I wasn't afraid of anything and was really safer there than if I'd been in town. When the next mail day rolled around, I saddled the horses and went to Soldier Bar to meet the plane and Dick.

It was after Dick's trip to town that we decided to find out about the building we'd seen up river. We took a lunch and the dogs and set off early in the morning. When we came to the cabin we found it was the Bernard Creek Guard Station.

That was as far as we went that day. A few days later Dick decided to make a fast trip by himself and see if he could find anything beyond the guard station. This time he found the Flying B Ranch. He crossed the river to the ranch and it wasn't long before he had gotten acquainted and hired out for a winter's job. He was in high spirits when he returned to camp that night.

The time was winding down at Waterfall and Dick had other places and things to plan for. We contacted Bob Fogg again and told him I would be flying out on his next trip. I would go to Slate Creek and Dick would take the stock, the dogs, his duffel and bedroll and go to the Flying B. All camp gear went with Dick also.

So ended a wonderful summer on the Middle Fork of the Salmon River and our camp at Waterfall. We had been there three months. I loaded my gear and drove to Slate Creek. Going through Riggins, I stopped off at Summerville's and asked Velma for a job. I would need one until Dick sent for me. Nothing had been said about me going in. That would be settled later.

Again I was at home, working part time in Riggins and

getting on with my life. About two months after Dick went to the Flying B, I was allowed to go in for a while. Since I wasn't working there I could only stay so long. All that winter I flew in and out whenever I could. I was getting to be a seasoned flier. The airstrip at the Flying B was a big one compared to the postage stamp airfields I'd been landing on. It was probably a half mile from the ranch. So passed a winter and spring, and when summer came and they were having more and more guests, I was hired.

THE FLYING B RANCH

The Flying B Ranch was a corporation. People bought memberships, then paid for their stay at the ranch when they flew in. That was their way of paying for the upkeep of the ranch. Also, guests were invited in to take advantage of the accommodations that were offered.

It was a beautiful place. The president at that time was Marty Rust. Bill and Marie Sullivan were the managers. When Dick was hired he was to be the packer. There were many other chores he had to do as well. He kept the horses and mules shod and during the summer he set up hunting camps, cut wood, and made sure there was a convenient place at each camp to get water. The first winter he would be busy getting acquainted with the new country.

They had a woman hired permanently as a helper in the kitchen. That was all the help they needed after the busy season was over, so I was not hired on. I could only stay for a couple of weeks, then I would return to Slate Creek. At home I was busy getting caught up on leather orders I had taken and with work at Summerville's in Riggins. The fall, winter, and spring passed very quickly. Seemed like I was either flying into or flying out of the Flying B. It was really an exciting lifestyle. I flew with Ed Osterman, a very good bush pilot. He landed at the Slate Creek emergency field so I didn't have to drive from McCall after being in the back country.

*Bill and Marie Sullivan. The Sullivans, shown
here with their son Terry, were managers at
the Flying B Ranch.*

When summer rolled around, Marty Rust decided to
get some redbone hounds so that guests who wanted to
go on a cougar or bear hunt would have a new experience.
Dick trained them with our dogs and they worked well
together.

One time, after staying two weeks, instead of calling for
a plane, we decided I should fly out to Boise on the mail
plane then get another plane to take me to Slate Creek.

When the mail plane came, I got in and we left for Boise,
stopping at different small ranches along the Middle
Fork. At one of these stops, the pilot noticed we were

getting a flat tire. I wondered what he was going to do. Then I watched him take a package of chewing gum out of his pocket, unwrap each stick, and put it all in his mouth. After he had chewed it up well, he placed it on the leak on the tire, covered it with duct tape, pumped up the tire, and took off. We made several more landings and arrived at the Boise airport without mishap. It had been a little unnerving at each landing, but the pilot was calm. He must have had that experience before.

At Boise another plane was arranged for me to fly to Slate Creek. We again buzzed the house where Dick's folks were living and Dick's dad came to pick me up.

There was always plenty of work to do at home, wood and water to pack every day and a trip to White Bird to get the mail. I washed and ironed and just enjoyed being home. I never knew how long it would be until I returned to the ranch.

This summer, as more and more guests and members began to fly into the ranch, they decided to hire me. Dick

Babe and her colt. Babe, Dick's saddle horse, gave birth to this filly colt at the Flying B ranch.

wrote that I should get my things ready to come in. That meant taking care of the house and making it secure before leaving. I had no idea when I would be back.

My job at the Flying B was domestic--washing dishes, cleaning cabins, doing laundry, and helping in the kitchen when needed. I would also serve tables when there were more guests than could be seated in the kitchen and the dining room had to be set up.

I had my own horse at the ranch because we had our own horses and mules there. When my work was finished and I had a few hours to spare, I could ride with Dick or go off by myself to explore the country. I was always on the lookout for old tepee holes and arrowheads. Nothing much was ever found, by me, anyway.

During the hottest part of the summer, planes were not supposed to fly into the ranch during the middle of the day. It is extremely dangerous to try to land in the canyon when the temperature is close to 100 degrees.

One afternoon we heard a plane and couldn't believe anyone would be flying into the canyon at that time. But sure enough, it was preparing to land. We never knew exactly what happened, but we heard the crash. We all grabbed emergency blankets and equipment that was ready for such things and raced across the footbridge to where it had crashed into the mountain. I was half afraid to get too close in case it burst into flames. Bill and Dick were there first. All were safely taken from the plane; no one was killed. Of course, there were a few bumps and bruises, but they were four lucky people.

It was very exciting. Phone calls were made to the aeronautics people. Although it hadn't caused any deaths it had to be reported. There were many things to be taken care of by the people involved. Their plane was demolished. Another plane came to get them the next day and their visit to the ranch was shorter than they had planned. There was never another accident while we were there. Thank goodness. One was enough.

When fall came, Dick had lined up some people to go to the Waterfall area to hunt elk. We packed our own camp back to Waterfall Campground where we had camped before. That was such a great place to camp. It was like going home. All the hunters were very pleased, even though it was quite a ride to get there. All filled their tags and the hunt was a success. We took down the camp and packed it back to the ranch since we had no more parties coming to this camping spot. After the hunting season I returned to Slate Creek. There was no work for extra help at this time of year. I got a part-time job at Summerville's and started getting some of my old jobs caught up.

When December came Dick wrote that Bill and Marie and their son, Terry, were going out for the holidays and I was to come in and help run the place. I called for a plane, but when it tried to land at the Flying B, the strip was fogged in and we had to fly on to Boise. There the weather stayed socked in for three days. Finally, on Christmas morning, it cleared. Bill, Marie, and Terry were waiting to go out.

The weather turned very cold. It was a chore keeping the fires going in the buildings that had running water. We noticed more and more ice forming on the river. After a week we walked down to the river and it was frozen over enough to walk on. I tried it out just so far but didn't trust the ice.

They kept a team of draft horses to use when feeding stock in the winter. Each day we harnessed the team, drove to the haystack, loaded the wagon with hay, and fed the animals.

Though we'd been told there would be no guests, a few flew in after New Year's Eve. Then Dick somehow injured his back and was laid up for the remainder of the time the Sullivans were gone. I not only had my work to do but his as well. I groaned every time I heard an airplane. I had plenty to do without guests to cook for, too.

I enjoyed feeding because I liked to drive the team. Thank goodness Dick had taught me how to harness the team and hook them to the wagon or I don't know what I would have done. Getting the bales of hay off the stack was the hardest, but I got the job done. After the Sullivans returned, I stayed on for a few weeks longer to help Dick with his work.

When Dick was able to do for himself, I decided to fly to Slate Creek. There wasn't that much to do now that it was wintertime and the Sullivans were back to take over.

I wasn't home more than a few days when word was radioed to Boise and relayed by phone that I was to fly back right away. A plane would be at Slate Creek at a given time. Things sometimes move pretty fast.

Bill had suddenly announced that he and Marie were quitting. They had gotten another job. Terry was nearly school age and they would have to think about his education. Dick and I were asked to manage the ranch until someone could be found to take over.

ANOTHER DISASTER AT SLATE CREEK

The new managers had just gotten settled in when we received a message of a disaster at Slate Creek. We needed to fly out as soon as possible. We radioed for a plane and left the next day. When we flew over the place we couldn't believe our eyes. What a terrible sight we saw. Very high water had caused massive damage.

Chandler's bridge, which was made of log stringers with wood planking, had come loose and floated down-stream, lodging in the narrowest part of the creek just above the lower house. No work had been done on this particular part of the creek. When debris piled up behind the bridge, the water built up and cut a new channel. It headed right for the house and outbuildings. As debris piled up around the buildings, more water built up. Dick's folks told us what had happened, since we weren't there at the peak of the flood.

Muddy water had seeped in around the front door and, since it was a cement floor, rose and soaked everything, ruining a lot of things. When the water receded there was a mess to clean up, inside and out. The folks had a freezer in the tack shed and the water ruined that. Since we had two freezers, we gave them one of ours. The cellar was the only building that had no water in it. It had been built with thick, sawdust-filled walls and a very tight-fitting door.

I had borrowed a machine for sewing leather from a friend and left it behind the house when we moved. That, too, was washed down the creek into the Salmon River. I felt bad about that, as it didn't belong to me and I should have taken better care of it.

My car had been left at the folk's place too, and water had gotten into that, leaving mud caked inside. Also, the motor was covered with mud. When it was cleaned out, we took bets as to whether it would run or not. Dick turned on the key and after a few tries the motor purred like a kitten. You just can't beat a Chevy.

We tried to get the U.S. Corps of Engineers again to help us repair our land, but since we were the only ones seriously damaged on the creek we had to be responsible for all expenses. We got Ted Taknen from Old Meadows again to bring his D-8 caterpillar down to do some more creek work. This was going to be another big job.

We had no more soil or rocks to use as fill so we had to have that hauled in. Just another added expense. Not much was left now to wash away. Hopefully this would be the last of the disasters. But that was what we'd thought the last time. Living along a creek was getting to be a bad deal, for us anyway.

We had to tell Ted just what we wanted him to do as we had to leave and go back to the Flying B. We left, but our thoughts remained at home. When the weather warmed up and the snows melted in the high country, we would quit our job. We'd trail our stock to Big Creek and have a truck meet us.

We'd had another interesting job and met many new people. One of the couples we met, Ray and Jan Seal, would help us with a job in the future. We'd been gone over two years and it was time to take care of our place.

Dick's folks went to Boise for a few days and while they were gone I scrubbed and cleaned all the log walls that had been damaged by high water, wondering how many other things could happen to us.

Then Dick had to make a trip to New Meadows. There was a short in the wiring in his pickup but he didn't know it. When he turned off the motor, it burst into flames. He jumped out, but before any help could arrive, the truck was destroyed. After that, Dick took over my car.

We both went to work at Summerville's on the same shift. Dick tended bar and I waited tables in the restaurant when needed and served as a cocktail waitress three nights a week.

That year we enjoyed having Thanksgiving dinner at Summervilles. They closed the restaurant and bar around noon and all employees and their families had dinner together. It was a very warm and generous thing for them to do.

After the Christmas holidays, Dick decided we'd be going another direction for work. In early spring we traded in my car for a brand new pickup. It was our first and only new pickup.

SUN VALLEY

This time we were heading for Sun Valley in central Idaho. Ray and Jan Seal were working there. Dick had a job at the stables situated halfway between Sun Valley and Ketchum.

We made a trip to Sun Valley to see what things we would need to take with us. There was no housing at the stables but there was space where a trailer had been. We got a room and the next day left for Boise where we purchased a 28-foot trailer to live in. We had it hauled to Sun Valley and set in place. Then we returned home, loaded the new pickup with everything we would need, and closed the house. We left our dogs at Slate Creek with Dick's folks and thus a new adventure began.

Talk about uptown living — running water, a bathroom, electric lights, heat. Boy, this was high style. Eventually we had a telephone put in, the first we'd ever had.

Dick was working for Ray Seal. There were trail rides, hay rides in the summer, and sleigh rides in the winter. It was going to be a new experience for Dick. He was around horses but there would be no packing.

Needing an extra man, Dick asked Ray to hire a friend of ours from the Salmon River. So Gail Wright came to work. He was to be a guide for the trail riders. There was a small, one-man trailer set up near the barn for him to live in. He ate his meals with us and I did his laundry in

220

Ketchum with ours.

When we got settled in, I started looking for work. Not having any office experience, I began babysitting for people who lived at the Sun Valley Lodge. It was good pay, $1.75 an hour or $1.60 an hour per additional child if there were more than one in the family. Two children amounted to $3.35 and that was good money.

Still, I kept looking for something better and it wasn't long until one of the people Dick met at the Flying B asked me if I would like to work in the accounting office in Sun Valley. After stating I had no experience, she asked me if I knew the alphabet. I said sure, and she said I had the job. I was hired over other applicants because I had no experience. I was taught to work the Bill Janns way. Janns was owner of the Sun Valley complex.

I worked in bills payable and after I had been working for six weeks I was the only one of thirteen office workers to receive a raise. I felt real good about that and tried to learn all I could. After a few months I worked one day a month in payroll helping a very nice lady named Coy Grace. For someone who knew nothing about office work, I was doing a very important job.

Dick was pleased with his job, so things were going very well. This was the first time we had a home where we could have a telephone. I went with Dick as much as I could on the evening rides. We lived close to the skating rink and could hear the music every evening.

This was another outstanding place. Every place we had been had its own charm. The summer seemed to disappear into fall and winter. The skiing season came with lots of snow and cold. Sleigh rides started. I went in the sleigh as often as possible because Dick always let me drive the team back from Trail Creek Lodge. The paying guests didn't seem to mind when I took the reins and had a good time. The holidays came and went.

When spring came Dick wasn't feeling too well so I went out to help Gail saddle the horses. Before I cooked breakfast, I would saddle about 25 head. Gail did all the wrangling. They must have had at least 40 or 50 head and many teams. It was a big job for one person, and I was always glad to help out. After helping with the saddling and getting breakfast over, I had to get myself ready to go to work. It made a long day.

By the time fall had ended Dick was talking of returning to Slate Creek. His health wasn't good and I think he was lonesome for the Snake and Salmon rivers. In time we moved the trailer to a trailer park in Ketchum and sold it, loaded our belongings into the pickup, and headed for home. When we quit, Gail did too, and rode with us. The next day we drove him to Grangeville.

Not very much time passed before we hired out to Bud again and were back on the Snake River.

ALBERT CRAWFORD

After returning to Slate Creek from Sun Valley, we found things changed at home. Having Dick's folks living so close caused complications. Dick decided we'd go back to the Snake River. We packed, saddled up, and rode over the rim to Kirkwood. It was late in October.

Again I found myself doing the cooking at Kirkwood. There had been a lot of changes while we were gone. The lovely, big Monarch range was gone and in its place was a new propane stove. Beside it sat a new water heater. A small propane heating stove was just inside the kitchen door on the left as you entered. The nice, big kerosene refrigerator was gone and a new propane one took its place. Two lights had been added.

Outside, the meat house was still there and so was the old garden spot on the east side of the house near the ditch. The bunkhouse looked great. The big lilac bush remained, as did the trees on the east side of the house. A huge propane tank had been added — some old and some new.

It was a shock to see the Snake River running clear. We were used to muddy water. We noticed in time that the fishing wasn't as good as it had once been. Then we began to notice that the sand bars were getting smaller and the driftwood we depended on was no longer available. We had used all that was around and, since there was no more high water, there was no driftwood. Too many

changes had come. I was grateful to have the opportunity
to live on the Snake River before the dams were built. The
river flowed the same, the mountains stayed the same,
but there was a big difference; there was a feeling of
newness.

That winter Dick built a stockade corral across the
creek beyond the Hannah cabin. We went through
another lambing and shearing season and nothing much
had changed as far as work was concerned. I got to go
with Dick quite a few times when he packed supplies up
the river.

But the summer would be a little different for me. When
lambing was over, I rode with Dick, taking a herder
named Albert Crawford and his band of sheep through
the Seven Devils Mountains to New Meadows for shipping.

Each year, Albert brought his sheep in for shearing
from Lightning Creek where he had wintered, arriving at
Kirkwood about February 15th. When his band was
sheared, he trailed back out of the immediate area until
time to come back to Kirkwood for lambing, about the
tenth of March.

After his band lambed, he began moving the sheep
south along the canyon face to Willow Creek, Sheep
Creek, and on to Low Saddle. He would stay at Low
Saddle until about the 10th of June and sometimes as
late as the 15th. This year, Dick and I joined him at Low
Saddle and began moving his camp through the mountains.

From Low Saddle we went to McGaffee Camp, then on
to Old Timer, arriving around July 1st. We left for Windy
Saddle seven days later. What a fun summer!

Albert would take his two dogs and leave camp by
daylight to start trailing his sheep. We would pack up the
camp, go to the next campsite, and set up. Albert would

Albert Crawford herded sheep for Bud Wilson during the time Dick and I were working for Bud. This photo was taken in later years at his home on the Salmon River. (Photo by Verna Slane)

225

come in around 10 a.m. for breakfast. After he had eaten he would go back out with his sheep and stay until he had bedded them down for the night.

I liked the idea of a new camp every few days. There wasn't anything to do other than cook the meals and do the washing when we were going to stay long enough to get it dry. I was learning to knit and was knitting myself a sweater, white with a red and black pattern. It was fancy, but by the time I got to Heaven's Gate, the white part was almost as black as the black part. I tried to keep it clean, but the dust made it impossible. After it was finished, washed and blocked it was really pretty.

It was late one evening at Heaven's Gate, after we had set up camp and Albert had come in for supper, that Bud and his son-in-law showed up. They had brought with them a small TV-radio. The screen on the TV was probably three by four inches. We all took turns watching the first man land on the moon.

The next morning, as I prepared to continue on through with Dick and Albert, I found I had to go back with Bud. His son-in-law was going in my place.

Dick took Albert and the herd on to the West Fork of the Rapid River (this took two days), then on to Frog Pond, Iron Phone on Kern Hill, Star Butte, Lick Creek, and finally New Meadows.

I went to New Meadows with Bud where he had work to do. I stayed with Lois McCune, owner of the New Meadows Hotel and Bar. Before long the herders were all in and the sheep were at the stockyards. The lambs were ready to ship. I cooked for all the herders in Lois's kitchen. After the shipping, Dick packed sheep camps back to the Snake River to their winter range.

After Dick had gone, I caught a ride to Slate Creek where I got the truck and went on to Grangeville. The next day, the 1st of October, I had gall bladder surgery.

A month later, Dick came up from the Snake River and said I had to ride back in with him. It would be too late if I waited any longer. So, less than a month from surgery, I got on my horse and rode 27 miles from Slate Creek to Kirkwood. That was one miserable trip, especially the downhill. Was I ever glad to see the Kirkwood house.

The next day, instead of riding my horse to Sheep Creek, I caught the mail boat. Dick took my saddlehorse with the pack string. We would be living at Sheep Creek this winter.

When it was time for lambing and shearing, Dick went alone. I stayed right where I was. I was glad someone else was cooking. I took care of the dogs and my horse, cleaned trail, and fished. Great life!

When April came, we packed up our belongings and headed back to the Salmon River and home. Dick was again self-employed. We decided to stay at home as much as possible that summer. There were many things to be done. When fall came, Dick and a friend decided to hunt up Slate Creek.

GETTING EVEN

The death of my dog really hurt. I guess that's why I wanted to get even with Dick some way and was always looking for ways.

Dick and a friend were going to hunting camp. I was supposed to pack a camp while Dick and his friend shod and saddled the stock. A pressure cooker is a must in camp, especially in the high country. When we were in town I had forgotten to buy a new sealing ring for the pressure cooker. So when I started packing for their camp and remembered the ring, I had a bright idea. This was one time I could get even with Dick. I just put the lid on the cooker, and put it in the camp box. I knew he was going to use it to make a stew that night. Dick was a good camp cook. He had taken meat from the freezer and plenty of vegetables. I knew when he discovered the ring missing, the hunting camp would resound with all kinds of cuss words. He would be livid with rage.

I was several miles down the country from him, so I was safe for the time being. That was really a very mean thing to do, as I knew how important it was to have the cooker. The day would come when they returned from hunting. I thought about that day, but by then the worst of his fury would be over.

I did feel guilty after they left, but not guilty enough to get in the pickup and go to camp. I would have had to walk several miles from the end of the road, and I wasn't that eager to make amends. Not quite yet. I was getting to be rather cruel in some things I did. Always trying to get even, and always losing out in the long run. Made things mighty interesting, though, with never a dull moment.

Then I decided I'd better do something nice for him to kinda' smooth things over. So I made him some new shirts. He always picked out his own materials and if he had a nice, new shirt it might off-set the mean thing I'd done.

Well, I won't go into detail about what happened when he returned, except it wasn't as bad as I thought it would be. He was mad all right, but the fury had worn off.

On the way back down the creek Dick had found an old Forest Service sign that had "Freedom" on it. He brought it home, whittled it down, and kept just the name "Freedom," which was what Slate Creek used to be called. He hung the sign inside the house over the front door. He said the house reminded him of his freedom.

After the meat had been taken care of, we packed up and headed for the Snake River.

THE SNAKE RIVER, LAST TIME

There was always plenty of work to do at the Kirkwood ranch: supplies to pack to camps, extra supplies to be left at Sheep Creek and Squaw Creek. The name of Squaw Creek has been changed to Bernard Creek, but to me it will always be Squaw Creek. That's where we had many a fun overnight stay with Pick and Lillie.

This would be our last winter on the Snake River. It's a good thing we don't know what the future is going to bring. Everything changes but life goes on.

When we went to the Snake River to build the bunkhouse for Bud there had been only a very small one-room bunkhouse on the south side of the house next to the irrigation ditch. Dick tore that down before he started on the new one.

Bud did many things on the ranch. He was the one who had the road built down Kirkwood Creek. He put in the lambing sheds, grain bins, new fencing, and things that made work on the ranch more efficient. He was the one who pioneered early lambing and shearing on the Snake River. Everyone said it would never work, but it did.

When the Hells Canyon National Recreation Area was established, the bunkhouse was not the required fifty years old to meet the antiquity regulations for preserving buildings in the area. The following is what the Forest Service has written about the bunkhouse we built in 1952:

Structure No. 13-B, built in 1952, does not meet the 50-year-old criteria; however, the structure is architecturally unique in design and detail. It is extremely well made, and the attention paid to construction detail is superb. Most who visit the site consider the Sterling Cabin to be a local historic landmark. The cabin is given considerable attention in the well known book, *Snake River of Hells Canyon*, (Carrey, et al). For these reasons, the cabin can be considered to have both local and regional historical significance.

(Re-printed with the permission of Ed Cole, Hells Canyon National Recreation Area Ranger.)

The Kirkwood stockade corral. This stockade was built by Dick in the early 1960s near the Hanah Cabin at Kirkwood.

THE STERLING YEARS

Dick was an expert with an axe, and it showed in his work. The building is now registered in the National Historical Records in Washington, D.C. What an honor! Bud Wilson can also be proud of it as it was through him that we had a chance to build it.

It is strange that, as I look back, the rough, sad times are stronger in my memory than the good, happy times. There must be a reason for that. There have been times we played as hard as we worked, because you can't just work all your life.

In this narrative, there have been as many years left out as have been written about. Some highlights of different years have been put together so as not to be repetitive. The work on the Snake River was about the same every time. Naturally, there were a few changes, as on any ranch. I can still remember times being with Dick and the pack string and dogs, but I can't remember just where we were. I remember one time being in the mountains, and when we camped for the night we picked a spot near a mountain stream where there were lots of down, dead logs. Dick took the chainsaw and cut and skidded the logs to a fairly level spot and build a log frame of four logs for a tent frame. That way we only had to stretch our tent over the temporary frame. We burned the chips and squaw wood around the campsite and left it clean. What we were doing at the time I can't remember, but I do remember what happened to our campsite. It wasn't good. The Forest Service came along and took down our log frames. Too bad. They would have made nice spots for some hunter during the hunting season.

Dick was a fanatic about his camp and his camp equipment. Everything had to be just the very best. We had top-notch camp equipment. Our stove was specially made to Dick's specifications. It was a super stove. Our griddle was magnesium instead of heavy iron, as it was

232

easier to pack. We had matching heavy plastic dishes and the best of cooking utensils. Nothing was too good. We always had folding camp chairs if we were alone, and cut blocks of wood for chairs at hunting camps. In later years we used folding lawn chairs for all in the party. Every sheepherder's camp, as well as ours, had at least one foot stool, which fit nicely in one of the camp boxes. Dick designed the camp boxes that were used in the kitchen tent and had them made. Also he made the lathe canvas table and work counter. It was easy to cut poles for legs and log frame. Rolled up, they took very little space in the camp.

Dick was really a very remarkable man. He wanted to live as free as his horses and dogs. But as the years passed, I became a dreamer. Maybe I always had been. I could see so many things that could be done with Slate Creek and realized, as the years passed, that this place that was to be a perfect home for us, turned out to be, in some ways, just the opposite.

I got to spending time watching clouds and thinking how it should have been. But then, again, maybe how things happened were exactly how they were supposed to. None of my dreams came true. The second house was never finished. It was beautiful on the inside, but the water system was never put in. And if we lived there fifty years, it would never have changed. That, in itself, is a small issue. Just another dream that disappeared along the way.

I have no complaints about my life though. I certainly learned a lot, and wouldn't change it if I could. I would do some things differently, but probably something else would have taken its place. Life can take some strange twists.

Since Dick's death, I have lived in Enterprise, Oregon. I work for the Hells Canyon National Recreation Area. It has been a difficult task writing down what I could remember and I have many people to thank for all the help and encouragement they have given me.

It was over twenty years ago that I started writing down some of the places we had been. I put it aside to do more at a later date. I remembered it about five years ago and decided it was time to finish it. I miss the times in the back country, riding the trails and the way we camped Sometimes, at certain times of the year, I can remember what we were doing and the fun we had doing it. There was not much time to become bored with anything at that time.

I have returned to the Snake River many times and always enjoy seeing the bunkhouse again. It is different there now. Green grass grows all around where, at the time we lived there, the grass was sparse. The bunkhouse, now the museum, is visited by many hundreds of people each year.

I go on a float trip every year with Canyon Outfitters of Halfway, Oregon, and relate stories to the others in the party about life before the dams were built, when the only people on the river were the ones who worked on the ranches in that particular part of the country.

Certain times of the year, or when the clouds roll up in an unusual way, I think about another time in the past that reminds me of being on the trail somewhere. Not many people have had the chance to learn and live and be places and travel as much as I have. It has been what is called, "A Wonderful Life."